THE WISDOM OF THE ANCIENTS,

AND

NEW ATLANTIS.

CASSELL'S NATIONAL LIBRARY.

THE

WISDOM OF THE ANCIENTS

AND

NEW ATLANTIS.

BY

FRANCIS BACON.

CASSELL & COMPANY, LIMITED:

LONDON, PARIS, NEW YORK & MELBOURNE.

1886.

INTRODUCTION.

FRANCIS BACON'S *Wisdom of the Ancients* was written in Latin—*De Sapientia Veterum Liber*—and first published as a small volume in 1609. The translation here given was made in Bacon's lifetime, by Sir Arthur Gorges, or Gorge (the name was written either way by those who bore it), and published ten years after the appearance of the original. The translator was of the family of Sir Ferdinando Gorges, Governor of Plymouth, who, from the year 1605 until his death in 1647, was active in favouring the colonisation of New England, and in 1635 was made the first Governor of Massachusetts under the English Crown, to which the Council of New England had then surrendered its powers. A grandson of Sir Ferdinando was that other Ferdinando, not a knight, who published in 1659 a description of New England, under the name of *America Painted to the Life*. The only publication of Sir Arthur Gorges', besides this translation of *The Wisdom of the Ancients*, had relation to the subject that most occupied the attention of his family, being a *Transcript, etc., relating to an Office called the Public Register for General Commerce.*

Bacon wrote this book at the age of forty-eight, four years after the publication of his *Two Books of the Advancement of Learning,* the first important work of the series that set forth his philosophy of Nature, and three years before the publication of the second edition (enlarged in its contents from ten to thirty-eight) of the *Essays,* that set forth his philosophy of Human Life.

Bacon's *New Atlantis,* written at the age of sixty-three, in the days of his withdrawal from all public office, and about two years before his death, at Highgate, on the 9th of April, 1626, was not published until the year after his death. It is unfinished, but nearly finished. Solon was said to have been writing in his last days of a perfect island of Atlantis. Plato, in his unfinished *Critias,* left part of a sketch of an ideal conflict, by citizens of an ideal Athens, with invaders from a vast island of Atlantis, fabled to be where America long afterwards was found; and Bacon placed his New Atlantis in another island continent, fabled to be where Australia has since been found. Like his *Wisdom of the Ancients,* Bacon's *New Atlantis* was written and first published in Latin. The English version here given appeared in 1629, as an appendix to Bacon's *Sylva Sylvarum, or Natural History in Ten Centuries.* It is of especial interest as Bacon's suggestion of a world in which that experimental study of nature, which he chiefly lived to promote, raised to a nobler height the life of man.

H. M.

TO THE

HIGH AND ILLUSTRIOUS PRINCESS

THE LADY ELIZABETH

OF GREAT BRITAIN,

Duchess of Bavaria, Countess Palatine of the Rhine,
and Chief Electress of the Empire.

MADAM,—Among many the worthy Chancellors of
this famous Isle, there is observed in Sir Thomas More
and Sir Francis Bacon an admirable sympathy of wit
and humour : witness those grave monuments of invention and learning wherewith the world is so plentifully enriched by them both. I will instance only in
the conceived *Utopia* of the one, and the revealed
Sapientia Veterum of the other : whereof the first,
under a mere idea of perfect State government, contains an exact discovery of the vanities and disorders
of real countries; and the second, out of the folds
of poetical fables, lays open those deep philosophical
mysteries which had been so long locked up in the
casket of antiquity; so that it is hard to judge to
whether of these two worthies policy and morality is
more beholding. I make no question, therefore, but

this observation (touching the parallel of their spirits) shall pass so current to succeeding ages, that it will be said of them, as in former times pronounced of Xenophon and Plato, "Fuere æquales."

And for this book that I humbly present to your Highness, which so eminently expresseth its own perfection, in me it would seem no less a vanity to give it attributes of glory and praise, than if I should lend spectacles to Lynx, or an eye to Argus; knowing it needless to waste gilding on pure gold, which is ever best valued by its own true touch and lustre. But to descend to myself, that do now lay before your princely censure the translation of these excellent and judicious discourses, so barely wrapping up in my harsh English phrase that which the author so richly attired in a sweet Latin style, I must therein fly to the sanctuary of your gracious acceptance. In which hope securing my doubts, I do with all reverence kiss your princely hands, remaining ever ready to approve myself

Your Highness'

Most dutiful and most devoted Servant,

ARTHUR GORGES.

TO THE BOOK.

Rich mine of art : minion of Mercury ;
True touchstone of the mind of Mystery ;

Invention's storehouse : Nymph of Helicon :
Deep Moralist of Time's tradition :—

Unto this Paragon of Brutus' race
Present thy service, and with cheerful grace

Say (if Pythagoras believed may be),
The soul of Ancient Wisdom lives in thee.

PREFACE.

———◦———

THE antiquities of the first age (except those we find in Sacred Writ) were buried in oblivion and silence: silence was succeeded by poetical fables; and fables again were followed by the records we now enjoy. So that the mysteries and secrets of antiquity were distinguished and separated from the records and evidences of succeeding times by the veil of fiction, which interposed itself, and came between those things which perished and those which are extant. I suppose some are of opinion, that my purpose is to write toys and trifles, and to usurp the same liberty in applying that the poets assumed in feigning; which I might do, I confess, if I listed, and with more serious contemplations intermix these things, to delight either myself in meditation, or others in reading. Neither am I ignorant how fickle and inconstant a thing fiction is, as being subject to be drawn and wrested any way, and how great the commodity of wit and discourse is, that is able to apply things well, yet so as never meant by the first authors. But I remember that this liberty

hath been lately much abused; in that many, to purchase the reverence of antiquity to their own inventions
and fancies, have for the same intent laboured to wrest
many poetical fables. Neither hath this old and common vanity been used only of late or now and then:
for even Chrysippus long ago did (as an interpreter of
dreams) ascribe the opinions of the Stoics to the
ancient poets; and more sottishly do the Chymics
appropriate the fancies and delights of poets in the
transformations of bodies, to the experiments of their
furnace. All these things, I say, I have sufficiently
considered and weighed, and in them have seen and
noted the general levity and indulgence of men's wits
about allegories. And yet for all this I relinquish not
my opinion. For, first, it may not be that the folly and
looseness of a few should altogether detract from the
respect due to the parables: for that were a conceit
which might savour of profaneness and presumption:
for religion itself doth sometimes delight in such veils
and shadows; so that whoso exempts them, seems
in a manner to interdict all commerce between things
divine and human. But concerning human wisdom
I do indeed ingenuously and freely confess, that I am
inclined to imagine, that under some of the ancient
fictions lay couched certain mysteries and allegories,
even from their first invention. And I am persuaded

(whether ravished with the reverence of antiquity, or because in some fables I find such singular proportion between the similitude and the thing signified; and such apt and clear coherence in the very structure of them, and propriety of names wherewith the persons or actors in them are inscribed and entitled) that no man can constantly deny, but this sense was in the authors' intent and meaning when they first invented them, and that they purposely shadowed it in this sort. For who can be so stupid and blind in the open light, as, when he hears how Fame, after the giants were destroyed, sprung up as their youngest sister, not to refer it to the murmurs and seditious reports of both sides, which are wont to fly abroad for a time after the suppressing of insurrections? or when he hears how the giant Typhon, having cut out and brought away Jupiter's nerves, which Mercury stole from him, and restored again to Jupiter, doth not presently perceive how fitly it may be applied to powerful rebellions, which take from princes their sinews of money and authority, but so, that by affability of speech, and wise edicts (the minds of their subjects being in time privily and as it were by stealth reconciled), they recover their strength again? or when he hears how (in that memorable expedition of the gods against the giants) the braying of Silenus's ass conduced much to the profligation of the giants, doth not confidently imagine that it was invented to show how the greatest enterprises of rebels are often-times dispersed with vain rumours and fears?

Moreover, to what judgment can the conformity and signification of names seem obscure? seeing Metis, the wife of Jupiter, doth plainly signify counsel; Typhon, insurrection; Pan, universality; Nemesis, revenge; and the like. Neither let it trouble any man, if sometimes he meet with historical narrations, or additions for ornament's sake, or confusion of times, or something transferred from one fable to another, to bring in a new allegory: for it could be no otherwise, seeing they were the inventions of men who lived in divers ages, and had also divers ends; some being ancient, others neoterical; some having an eye to things natural, others to moral.

There is another argument (and that no small one neither) to prove that these fables contain certain hidden and involved meanings, seeing some of them are observed to be so absurd and foolish in the very relation, that they show and as it were proclaim a parable afar off. For such tales as are probable, they may seem to be invented for delight, and in imitation of history. And as for such as no man would so much as imagine or relate, they seem to be sought out for other ends. For what kind of fiction is that, wherein Jupiter is said to have taken Metis to wife, and perceiving that she was with child, to have devoured her, whence himself conceiving, brought forth Pallas armed out of his head? Truly I think there was never dream so different to the course of cogitation, and so full of monstrosity, ever hatched in the brain of man. Above all things this prevails most with me, and is of singular moment—that many of these fables seem not to be invented of those by whom they are related and celebrated, as by Homer, Hesiod, and others: for if it were so, that they took beginning in that age and from those authors by whom they are delivered and brought to our hands, my mind gives me there could be no great or high matter expected or supposed to proceed from them in respect of these originals. But if with attention we consider the matter, it will appear that they were delivered and related as things formerly believed and received, and not as newly invented and offered unto us. Besides, seeing they are diversely related by writers that lived near about one and the selfsame time, we may easily perceive that they were common things, derived from precedent memorials: and that they became various by reason of the divers ornaments bestowed on them by particular relations. And the consideration of this must needs increase in us a great opinion of them, as not to be accounted either the effects of the times or inventions of the poets, but as sacred relics or abstracted airs of better times, which by tradition from more ancient nations fell into the trumpets and flutes of the Grecians. But if any do obstinately contend that allegories are always adventitiously, and as it were by constraint, never naturally and properly included in fables, we will not be much troublesome, but suffer them to enjoy that gravity of judgment which I am sure they affect, although indeed it be but lumpish and almost leaden. And if they be worthy to be taken notice of, we will begin afresh with them in some other fashion.

There is found among men (and it goes for current) a twofold use of parables, and those (which is more to be admired) referred to contrary ends, conducing as well to the folding up and keeping of things under a veil, as to the enlightening and laying open of obscurities. But omitting the former, rather than to undergo wrangling, and assuming ancient fables as things vagrant and composed only for delight, the latter must questionless still remain, as not to be wrested from us by any violence of wit, neither can any that is but meanly learned hinder, but it must absolutely be received, as a thing grave and sober, free from all vanity, and exceeding profitable and necessary to all sciences. This is it, I say, that leads the understanding of man by an easy and gentle passage through all novel and abstruse inventions which any way differ from common received opinions. Therefore, in the first ages when many human inventions and conclusions which are now common and vulgar were new and not generally known, all things were full of fables, enigmas, parables, and similes of all sorts: by which they sought to teach and lay open, not to hide and conceal knowledge, especially seeing the understandings of men were in those times rude and impatient, and almost incapable of any subtleties, such things only excepted as were the objects of sense: for as hieroglyphics preceded letters, so parables were more ancient than arguments. And in these days also, he that would illuminate men's minds anew in any old matter, and that not with disprofit and harshness, must absolutely take the same course, and use the help of similes. Wherefore, all that hath been said we will thus conclude: the Wisdom of the Ancients, it was either much or happy: much if these figures and tropes were invented by study and premeditation; happy if they, intending nothing less, gave matter and occasion to so many worthy meditations. As concerning my labours, if there be anything in them which may do good, I will on neither part count them ill bestowed, my purpose being to illustrate either antiquity, or things themselves.   Neither am I ignorant that this very subject hath been attempted by others : but, to speak as I think, and that freely, without ostentation, the dignity and efficacy of the thing is almost lost by these men's writings, though voluminous and full of pains, which, not diving into the depth of matters, but skilful only in certain commonplaces, have applied the sense of these parables to certain vulgar and general things, not so much as glancing at their true virtue, genuine propriety, and full depth.   I, if I be not deceived, shall be new in common things.   Wherefore, leaving such as are plain and open, I will aim at farther and richer matters.

THE TABLE.

———◦◦———

THE WISDOM OF THE ANCIENTS.

—◦◦◦—

I.

CASSANDRA, OR DIVINATION.

THE poets fable that Apollo, being enamoured of
Cassandra, was, by her many shifts and cunning
flights, still deluded in his desire; but yet fed on with
hope until such time as she had drawn from him the
gift of prophesying; and having by such her dissimu-
lation in the end attained to that which from the
beginning she sought after, she at last flatly rejected his
suit; who, finding himself so far engaged in his
promise as that he could not by any means revoke
again his rash gift, and yet inflamed with an earnest
desire of revenge, highly disdaining to be made the
scorn of a crafty wench, annexed a penalty to his
promise, to wit, that she should ever foretell the truth,
but never be believed. So were her divinations always
faithful, but at no time regarded; whereof she still
found the experience, yea, even in the ruin of her own
country, which she had often forewarned them of, but
they neither gave credit nor ear to her words. This
fable seems to intimate the unprofitable liberty of

untimely admonitions and counsels. For they that
are so overweened with the sharpness and dexterity
of their own wit and capacity, as that they disdain to
submit themselves to the documents of Apollo, the god
of harmony, whereby to learn and observe the method
and measure of affairs, the grace and gravity of discourse, the differences between the more judicious and
more vulgar ears, and the due times when to speak and
when to be silent, be they never so sensible and
pregnant, and their judgments never so profound and
profitable, yet in all their endeavours, either of persuasion or perforce, they avail nothing, neither are
they of any moment to advantage or manage matters,
but do rather hasten on the ruin of all those that they
adhere or devote themselves unto. And then at last,
when calamity hath made men feel the event of neglect,
then shall they too late be reverenced as deep, foreseeing, and faithful prophets. Whereof a notable instance is eminently set forth in Marcus Cato Uticensis,
who, as from a watch-tower, discovered afar off, and
as an oracle long foretold, the approaching ruin of his
country and the plotted tyranny hovering over the
State, both in the first conspiracy, and as it was prose-
cuted in the civil contention between Cæsar and
Pompey; and did no good the while, but rather harmed
the commonwealth, and hastened on his country's bane,
which M. Cicero wisely observed, and, writing to a
familiar friend, doth in these terms excellently de-
scribe : "Cato optime sentit, sed nocet interdum
Reipublicæ; loquitur enim tanquam in Republicâ

Platonis, non tanquam in fæce Romuli." "Cato," saith he, "judgeth profoundly, but in the meantime damnifies the State; for he speaks as in the commonwealth of Plato, and not as in the dregs of Romulus."

II.

TYPHON, OR A REBEL.

JUNO being vexed, say the poets, that Jupiter had begotten Pallas by himself without her, earnestly pressed all the other gods and goddesses, that she might also bring forth of herself alone without him; and having by violence and importunity obtained a grant thereof, she smote the earth, and forthwith sprang up Typhon, a huge and horrid monster. This strange birth she committed to a serpent, as a foster-father, to nourish it, who no sooner came to ripeness of years, but he provoked Jupiter to battle. In the conflict, the giant, getting the upper hand, took Jupiter upon his shoulders, carried him into a remote and obscure country, and, cutting out the sinews of his hands and feet, brought them away, and so left him miserably mangled and maimed. But Mercury, recovering these nerves from Typhon by stealth, restored them again to Jupiter. Jupiter, being again by this means corroborated, assaults the monster afresh, and at the first strikes him with a thunderbolt : from whose blood serpents are engendered. This monster at length fainting and flying, Jupiter casts on him the mount Ætna, and with the weight thereof crushes him.

This fable seems to point at the variable fortune of princes, and the rebellious insurrection of traitors in a State. For princes may well be said to be married to their dominions, as Jupiter was to Juno ; but it happens now and then, that being debauched by the long custom of empiring, and bending towards tyranny, they endeavour to draw all to themselves, and, contemning the counsel of their nobles and senators, hatch laws in their own brain—that is, dispose of things by their own fancy and absolute power. The people, repining at this, study how to create and set up a chief of their own choice. This project, by the secret instigation of the peers and nobles, doth for the most part take his beginning ; by whose connivance the Commons being set on edge, there follows a kind of murmuring or discontent in the State, shadowed by the infancy of Typhon, which being nursed by the natural pravity and clownish malignity of the vulgar sort, unto princes as infestuous as serpents, is again repaired by renewed strength, and at last breaks out into open rebellion, which, because it brings infinite mischiefs upon prince and people, is represented by the monstrous deformity of Typhon ; his hundred heads signify their divided powers ; his fiery mouths, their inflamed intents ; his serpentine circles, their pestilent malice in besieging; his iron hands, their merciless slaughters; his eagle's talons, their greedy rapines; his plumed body, their continual rumours, and scouts, and fears, and such-like. And sometimes these rebellions grow so potent, that princes are enforced—transported, as it were, by the rebels, and forsaking the chief seats and cities of the kingdom—to contract their power, and, being deprived of the sinews of money and majesty, betake themselves to some remote and obscure corner within their dominions; but in process of time, if they bear their misfortunes with moderation, they may recover their strength by the virtue and industry of Mercury; that is, they may, by becoming affable, and by reconciling the minds and wills of their subjects with grave edicts and gracious speech, excite an alacrity to grant aids and subsidies whereby to strengthen their authority anew. Nevertheless, having learned to be wise and wary, they will refrain to try the chance of fortune by war, and yet study how to suppress the reputation of the rebels by some famous action, which if it fall out answerable to their expectation, the rebels, finding themselves weakened, and fearing the success of their broken projects, betake themselves to some sleight and vain bravadoes, like the hissing of serpents, and at length, in despair, betake themselves to flight; and then, when they begin to break, it is safe and timely for kings to pursue and oppress them with the forces and weight of the kingdom, as it were with the mountain Ætna.

III.

THE CYCLOPS, OR THE MINISTERS OF TERROR.

THEY say that the Cyclops, for their fierceness and cruelty, were by Jupiter cast into hell, and there doomed to perpetual imprisonment; but Tellus persuaded Jupiter that it would do well, if, being set at liberty, they were set to forge thunderbolts; which being done accordingly, they became so painful and industrious, as that day and night they continued hammering out in laborious diligence thunderbolts and other instruments of terror. In process of time, Jupiter, having conceived a displeasure against Æsculapius, the son of Apollo, for restoring a dead man to life by physic, and concealing his dislike because there was no just cause of anger, the deed being pious and famous, secretly incensed the Cyclops against him, who without delay slew him with a thunderbolt. In revenge of which act, Apollo (Jupiter not prohibiting it) shot them to death with his arrows.

This fable may be applied to the projects of kings, who having cruel, bloody, and exacting officers, do first punish and displace them, and afterwards by the counsel of Tellus—that is, of some base and ignoble person—and by the prevailing respect of profit, they admit them into their places again, that they may have instruments in a readiness, if at any time there should need either severity of execution or acerbity of exaction. These servile creatures, being by nature cruel, and by their former fortune exasperated, and perceiving well what is expected at their hands, do show themselves wonderful officious in such kind of employments; but being too rash and precipitate in seeking countenance, and creeping into favour, do sometimes take occasion from the secret beckonings and ambiguous commands of their prince, to perform some hateful execution. But princes, abhorring the fact, and knowing well that they shall never want such kind of instruments, do utterly forsake them, turning them over to the friends and allies of the wronged, to their accusations and revenge, to the general hatred of the people, so that with great applause and prosperous wishes and exclamations towards the prince, they are brought, rather too late than undeservedly, to a miserable end.

IV.

NARCISSUS, OR SELF-LOVE.

THEY say that Narcissus was exceeding fair and beautiful, but wonderful proud and disdainful; wherefore, despising all others in respect of himself, he led a solitary life in the woods and chases, with a few followers, to whom he alone was all in all. Among the rest there follows him the nymph Echo. During his course of life, it fatally so chanced that he came to a clear fountain, upon the bank whereof he lay down to repose himself in the heat of the day. And having espied the shadow of his own face in the water, was so besotted and ravished with the contemplation and admiration thereof, that by no means possible he could be drawn from beholding his image in this glass; insomuch that, by continual gazing thereupon, he pined away to nothing, and was at last turned into a flower of his own name, which appears in the beginning of the spring, and is sacred to the infernal powers, Pluto, Proserpina, and the Furies.

This fable seems to show the dispositions and fortunes of those who, in respect either of their beauty or other gifts wherewith they are adorned and graced by nature, without the help of industry, are so far besotted in themselves, as that they prove the cause of their own destruction. For it is the property of men infected with this humour not to come much abroad, or to be conversant in civil affairs, especially seeing those that are in public place must of necessity encounter with many contempts and scorns, which may much deject and trouble their minds; and therefore they lead for the most part a solitary, private, and obscure life, attended on with a few followers, and such as will adore and admire them, and like an Echo flatter them in all their sayings, and applaud them in all their words. So that, being by this custom seduced and puffed up, and as it were stupefied with the admiration of themselves, they are possessed with so strange a sloth and idleness, that they grow, in a manner, benumbed and defective of all vigour and alacrity. Elegantly doth this flower, appearing in the beginning of the spring, represent the likeness of these men's dispositions, who in their youth do flourish and wax famous, but being come to ripeness of years, they deceive and frustrate the good hope that is conceived of them. Neither is it impertinent that this flower is said to be consecrated to the infernal deities, because men of this disposition become unprofitable to all human things. For whatsoever produceth no fruit of itself, passeth and vanisheth as if it never had been, like the way of a ship in the sea, that the ancients were wont to dedicate to the ghosts and powers below.

V.

STYX, OR LEAGUES.

THE oath by which the gods were wont to oblige themselves, when they meant to ratify anything so firmly as never to revoke it, is a thing well known to the vulgar, as being mentioned almost in every fable, which was when they did not invoke or call to witness any celestial majesty or divine power, but only the river Styx, that with crooked and meandry turnings encircleth the palace of the infernal Dis. This was held as the only solemn manner of their sacrament, and beside it not any other vow to be accounted firm and inviolable; and therefore the punishment to be inflicted, if any did perjure themselves, was, that for certain years they should be put out of commons, and not be admitted to the table of the gods.

This fable seems to point at the leagues and packs of princes, of which more truly than opportunely may be said, that be they never so strongly confirmed with the solemnity and religion of an oath, yet are they for the most part of no validity; insomuch that they are made rather with an eye to reputation, and report, and ceremony, than to faith, security, and effect. Moreover, add to these the bonds of affinity as the sacraments of nature, and the mutual deserts of each part, and you shall observe that with a great many, all these things are placed a degree under ambition and profit, and the licentious desire of domination; and so much the rather, because it is an easy thing for princes to defend and cover their unlawful desires and unfaithful vows with many outwardly seeming fair pretexts, especially seeing there is no umpire or moderator of matters concluded upon, to whom a reason should be tendered. Therefore there is one true and proper thing made choice of, for the confirmation of faith,

and that no celestial power neither, but it is indeed
Necessity, a great god to great potentates, the peril
also of State, and the communication of profit. As
for necessity, it is elegantly represented by Styx, that
fatal and irremeable river, and this godhead did Iphi-
crates the Athenian call to the confirmation of a League,
of whom, because he alone is found to speak plainly
that which many hide covertly in their breasts, it
would not be amiss to relate the words. He, observing
how the Lacedæmonians had thought upon and propounded divers cautions, sanctions, confirmations, and
bonds pertaining to Leagues, interposed thus : " *Unum
Lacedæmonii nobis vobiscum vinculum et securitatis
ratio esse possit : si plane demonstretis vos ea nobis
concessisse, et inter manus posuisse, ut vobis facultas
lœdendi nos si maxime velletis minime suppeditari
possit.*" " There is one thing, O Lacedæmonians, that
would link us unto you in the bond of amity, and be
the occasion of peace and security : which is, if you
would plainly demonstrate that you have yielded up
and put into our hands such things as that, would
you hurt us never so fain, you should yet be disfur-
nished of means to do it." If, therefore, the power
of hurting be taken away, or if by breach of league
there follow the danger of the ruin or diminution
of the State or tribute; then indeed the leagues
may be seen to be ratified and established, and as
it were confirmed by the sacrament of the Stygian
lake, seeing that it includes the fear of prohibition,
and suspension from the table of the gods, under

B—15

which name the laws and prerogatives, the plenty
and felicity of a kingdom, were signified by the
ancients.

VI.

PAN, OR NATURE.

THE ancients have exquisitely described Nature under
the person of Pan, whose origin they leave doubtful,
for some say thàt he was the son of Mercury; others
attribute unto him a far different beginning, affirming
him to be the common offspring of Penelope's suitors,
upon a suspicion that every one of them had to do
with her, which latter relation doubtless gave occasion
to some after writers to entitle this ancient fable with
the name of Penelope, a thing very frequent amongst
them when they apply old fictions to young persons
and names, and that many times absurdly and indis-
creetly, as may be seen here; for Pan being one of the
ancient gods, was long before the time of Ulysses and
Penelope. Besides, for her matronal chastity she was
held venerable by antiquity. Neither may we pre-
termit the third conceit of his birth, for some say that
he was the son of Jupiter and Hybris, which signifies
contumely or disdain. But howsoever begotten, the
Parcæ, they say, were his sisters. He is portrayed by

the ancients in this guise : on his head a pair of horns
that reach to heaven; his body rough and hairy, his
beard long and shaggy ; his shape biformed—above like
a man, below like a beast ; his feet like goats' hoofs :
and he bore these ensigns of his jurisdiction, to wit, in
his left hand a pipe of seven reeds, and in his right a
sheep-hook, or a staff crooked at the upper end, and his
mantle made of a leopard's skin. His dignities and
offices were these : he was the god of hunters, of
shepherds, and of all rural inhabitants ; chief president,
also, of hills and mountains, and next to Mercury, the
ambassador of the gods. Moreover, he was accounted
the leader and commander of the Nymphs, which were
always wont to dance the rounds and frisk about him ;
he was accosted by the Satyrs and the old Sileni. He
had power also to strike men with terrors, and those
especially vain and superstitious, which are termed
Panic fears. His acts were not many. For aught that
can be found in records, the chiefest was that he
challenged Cupid at wrestling, in which conflict he had
the foil.

The tale goes, too, that he caught the giant Typhon
in a net, and held him fast. Moreover, when Ceres,
grumbling and chafing that Proserpina was ravished,
had hid herself away, and that all the gods took pains,
by dispersing themselves into every corner, to find her
out, it was only his good hap, as he was hunting, to
light on her, and acquaint the rest where she was. He
presumed also to put it to the trial who was the better
musician, he or Apollo, and by the judgment of Midas,

was indeed preferred; but the wise judge had a pair of ass's ears privily chopped to his noddle for his sentence. Of his love tricks, there is nothing reported, or at least not much; a thing to be wondered at, especially being among a troop of gods so profusely amorous. This only is said of him, that he loved the nymph Echo, whom he took to wife, and one pretty wench more, called Syrinx, towards whom Cupid, in an angry and revengeful humour, because so audaciously he had challenged him at wrestling, inflamed his desire. Moreover, he had no issue, which is a marvel also, seeing the gods, especially those of the male kind, were very generative; only he was the reputed father of a little girl called Iambe, that with many pretty tales was wont to make strangers merry; but some think she was indeed the child of his wife Iambe. This, if any be, is a noble tale, as being laid out and weighted with the secrets and mysteries of nature.

Pan, as his name imports, represents and lays open the All of things, or Nature. Concerning his origin, there are only two opinions that go for current: for either he came of Mercury, that is, the Word of God, which the Holy Scriptures without all controversy affirm, and such of the philosophers as had any smack of divinity assented unto; or else from the confused seeds of things. For they that would have one simple beginning, refer it unto God; or if a material beginning, they would have it various in power. So that we may end the controversy with this distribution

—that the world took beginning either from Mercury or from the seeds of all things.

Virg. *Eclogue* 6.

" *Namque canebat uti magnum per inane coacta*
  Semina, terrarumque, animæque, marisque fuissent
  Et liquidi simul ignis : ut his exordia primis
  Omnia, et ipse tener mundi concreverit orbis."

" For rich-veined Orpheus sweetly did rehearse
  How that the seeds of fire, air, water, earth,
  Were all packed in the vast void universe :
  And how from these as firstlings all had birth,
  And how the body of this orbic frame
  From tender infancy so big became. "

But as touching the third conceit of Pan's origin, it seems that the Grecians, either by intercourse with the Egyptians, or one way or other, had heard something of the Hebrew mysteries ; for it points to the state of the world, not considered in immediate creation, but after the fall of Adam, exposed and made subject to death and corruption ; for in that state it was, and remains to this day, the offspring of God and sin. And therefore, all these three narrations concerning the manner of Pan's birth may seem to be true, if it be rightly distinguished between things and times. For this Pan, or Nature, which we respect, contemplate, and reverence more than is fit, took beginning from the Word of God by the means of confused matter, and the entrance of prevarication and corruption.   The Destinies may well be thought the sisters of Pan, or Nature, because the beginnings, and continuances, and corruptions, and depressions, and dissolutions, and eminences, and labours, and felicities of things, and all the chances which can happen unto anything, are linked with the chains of causes natural.

Horns are attributed unto him, because horns are broad at the root and sharp at the ends, the nature of all things being like a pyramid, sharp at the top.   For individual or singular things, being infinite, are first collected into species, which are many also; then from species into generals, by ascending, are contracted into things or notions more general, so that at length Nature may seem to be contracted into a unity. Neither is it to be wondered at, that Pan toucheth heaven with his horns, seeing the height of Nature or universal ideas do in some sort pertain to things Divine, and there is a ready and short passage from metaphysic to natural theology.

The body of Nature is elegantly and with deep judgment depicted hairy, representing the beams or operations of creatures: for beams are, as it were, the hairs and bristles of nature, and every creature is either more or less beamy, which is most apparent in the faculty of seeing, and no less in every virtue and operation that effectuates upon a distant object : whatsoever works upon anything afar off, that may rightly be said to dart forth rays or beams.

Moreover, Pan's beard is said to be exceeding long,

because the beams or influences of celestial bodies do operate and pierce farthest of all, and the sun, when his higher half is shadowed with a cloud, his beams breaking out in the lower, looks as if he were bearded.

Nature is also excellently set forth with a biformed body, with respect to the differences between superior and inferior creatures. For the one part, by reason of their pulchritude, and equability of motion, and constancy, and dominion over the earth and earthly things, is worthily set out by the shape of man; and the other part, in respect of their perturbations and unconstant motions, and therefore needing to be moderated by the Celestial, may be well fitted with the figure of a brute beast. This description of his body pertains also to the participation of species, for no natural being seems to be simple, but as it were participating and compounded of two. As, for example, man hath something of a beast; a beast something of a plant; a plant something of an inanimate body; so that all natural things are in very deed biformed—that is to say, compounded of a superior and inferior species.

It is a witty allegory, that same of the feet of a goat, by reason of the upward tending motion of terrestrial bodies towards the air and heaven; for the goat is a climbing creature, that loves to be hanging about the rocks and steep mountains. And this is done also in a wonderful manner, even by those things which are destinated to this inferior globe, as may manifestly appear in clouds and meteors.

The two ensigns which Pan bears in his hands do point, the one at harmony, the other at empiry: for the pipe consisting of seven reeds doth evidently demonstrate the consent and harmony and discordant concord of all inferior creatures, which is caused by the motion of the seven planets; and that of the sheep-hook may be excellently applied to the order of nature, which is partly right, partly crooked. This staff, therefore, or rod, is especially crooked in the upper end, because all the works of Divine Providence in the world are done in a far-fetched and circular manner, so that one thing may seem to be effected, and yet indeed a clean contrary brought to pass, as the selling of Joseph into Egypt, and the like. Besides, in all wise human government, they that sit at the helm do more happily bring their purposes about, and insinuate more easily into the minds of the people, by pretexts and oblique courses, than by direct methods; so that all sceptres and maces of authority ought in very deed to be crooked in the upper end.

Pan's cloak or mantle is ingeniously feigned to be the skin of a leopard, because it is full of spots: so the heavens are spotted with stars, the sea with rocks and islands, the land with flowers, and every particular creature also is for the most part garnished with divers colours about the superficies, which is, as it were, a mantle unto it. The office of Pan can be by nothing so lively conceived and expressed, as by feigning him to be the god of hunters: for every natural action, and so, by consequence, motion and progression, is nothing else but a hunting. Arts and sciences have their works, and human counsels their ends, which they earnestly hunt after. All natural things have either their food as a prey, or their pleasure as a recreation, which they seek for, and that in most expert and sagacious manner.

> " *Torva Leæna Lupum sequitur, Lupus ille Capellam ;*
> *Florentem cythisum sequitur lasciva Capella.*"

> "The hungry lioness, with sharp desire,
>   Pursues the wolf, the wolf the wanton goat :
> The goat, again, doth greedily aspire
>   To have the trefoil-juice pass down her throat."

Pan is also said to be the god of the country clowns, because men of this condition lead lives more agreeable unto Nature, than those that live in the cities and courts of princes, where Nature, by too much art, is corrupted : so as the saying of the poet (though in the sense of love) might be here verified :

> " *Pars minima est ipsa puella sui.*"

> "The maid so tricks herself with art,
>   That of herself she is least part."

He was held to be Lord President of the Mountains, because in high mountains and hills, Nature lays herself most open, and men are most apt to view and contemplation.

Whereas Pan is said to be (next unto Mercury) the

messenger of the gods, there is in that a Divine mystery contained, for next to the Word of God the image of the world proclaims the power and wisdom divine, as sings the sacred poet, Psalm xix. 1, " *Cœli enarrant gloriam Dei, atque opera manuum ejus indicat firmamentum.*" "The heavens declare the glory of God, and the firmament showeth the works of His hands."

The Nymphs—that is, the souls of living things, take great delight in Pan : for these souls are the delights or minions of Nature, and the direction or conduct of these Nymphs is with great reason attributed unto Pan, because the souls of all things living do follow their natural dispositions as their guides, and with infinite variety every one of them after his own fashion doth leap and frisk and dance with incessant motion about her. The Satyrs and Sileni also—to wit, youth and old age—are some of Pan's followers : for of all natural things there is a lively, jocund, and (as I may say) a dancing age, and an age again that is dull, bibbling and reeling. The carriages and disposition of both which ages, to some such as Democritus was (that would observe them duly) might peradventure seem as ridiculous and deformed as the gambols of the Satyrs, or the gestures of the Sileni.

Of those fears and terrors of which Pan is said to be the author, there may be this wise construction made, namely, that Nature hath bred in every living thing a kind of care and fear tending to the preservation of its

own life and being, and to the repelling and shunning
of all things hurtful. And yet Nature knows not how
to keep a mean, but always intermixes vain and empty
fears with such as are discreet and profitable; so that
all things, if their insides might be seen, would appear
full of Panic frights; but men, especially in hard and
fearful and divers times, are wonderfully infatuated
with superstition, which, indeed, is nothing else but a
Panic terror.

Concerning the audacity of Pan in challenging
Cupid at wrestling, the meaning of it is, that matter
wants no inclination and desire to the relapsing and
dissolution of the world into the old chaos, if her
malice and violence were not restrained and kept in
order by the prepotent unity and agreement of things,
signified by Cupid, or the god of love; and therefore
it was a happy turn for men and all things else,
that in that conflict Pan was found too weak, and
was overcome.

To the same effect may be interpreted his catching
of Typhon in a net: for, howsomever there may sometimes happen vast and unwonted tumours (as the name
of Typhon imports), either in the sea, or in the air, or in
the earth, or elsewhere, yet Nature doth entangle in an
intricate toil, and curb and restrain, as it were with a
chain of adamant, the excesses and insolences of these
kinds of bodies.

But forasmuch as it was Pan's good fortune to find
out Ceres as he was hunting, and thought little of it,
which none of the other gods could do, though they

did nothing else but seek her, and that very seriously, it gives us this true and grave admonition : that we expect not to receive things necessary for life and manners from philosophical abstractions, as from the greater gods, albeit they applied themselves to no other study, but from Pan—that is, from discreet observation and experience, and the universal knowledge of the things of this world, whereby, oftentimes even by chance, and as it were going a hunting, such inventions were lighted upon.

The quarrel he made with Apollo about music, and the event thereof, contains a wholesome instruction, which may serve to restrain men's reasons and judgments with the reins of sobriety from boasting and glorying in their gifts. For there seems to be a two-fold harmony or music : the one of Divine Providence, and the other of Human Reason. Now to the ears of mortals, that is, to human judgment, the administration of the world and the creatures therein, and the more secret judgments of God, sound very hard and harsh ; which folly, albeit it will be set out with asses' ears, yet, notwithstanding, these ears are secret, and do not openly appear, neither is it perceived or noted as a deformity by the vulgar.

Lastly, it is not to be wondered at that there is nothing attributed unto Pan concerning loves, but only his marriage with Echo : for the world, or Nature, doth enjoy itself, and in itself all things else. Now he that loves would enjoy something, but where there is enough there is no place left to desire. Therefore there can be no wanton love in Pan or the World, nor desire to obtain anything (seeing he is contented with himself), but only speeches, which, if plain, may be intimated by the nymph Echo, or, if more quaint, by Syrinx. It is an excellent invention, that Pan or the World is said to make choice of Echo only (above all other speeches or voices) for his wife, for that alone is true philosophy which doth faithfully render the very words of the world, and is written no otherwise than the world doth dictate, it being nothing else but the image or reflection of it, not adding anything of its own, but only iterates and resounds. It belongs, also, to the sufficiency or perfection of the world, that he begets no issue: for the world doth generate in respect of its parts, but in respect of the whole how can it generate, seeing without it there is no body? Notwithstanding all this, the tale of that tattling girl fathered upon Pan, may in very deed with great reason be added to the fable: for by her are represented those vain and idle paradoxes concerning the nature of things, which have been frequent in all ages, and have filled the world with novelties, fruitless if you respect the matter, changelings if you respect the kind, sometimes creating pleasure, sometimes tediousness with their overmuch prattling.

VII.

PERSEUS, OR WAR.

PERSEUS is said to have been employed by Pallas for the destroying of Medusa, who was very infestuous to the western parts of the world, and especially about the utmost coasts of Hyberia—a monster so dire and horrid, that only by her aspect she turned men into stones. This Medusa alone, of all the Gorgons, was mortal, the rest not subject to death. Perseus, therefore, preparing himself for this noble enterprise, had arms and gifts bestowed on him by three of the gods: Mercury gave him wings annexed to his heels, Pluto a helmet, Pallas a shield and a looking-glass. Notwithstanding, although he was thus furnished, he went not directly to Medusa, but first to the Greæ, which by the mother's side were sisters to the Gorgons. These Greæ from their birth were hoar-headed, resembling old women. They had but one only eye, and one tooth among them all, both which she that had occasion to go abroad was wont to take with her, and at her return to lay them down again. This eye and tooth they lent to Perseus: and so, finding himself thoroughly furnished for the effecting of his design, he hastened towards Medusa. Her he found sleeping, and yet durst not present himself with his face towards her, lest she should awake, but, turning his head aside, beheld her in Pallas's glass, and, by this means directing his blow, cut off her head, from whose blood gushing out instantly came Pegasus, the flying horse. Her head thus smit off, Perseus bestows on Pallas her shield, which yet retained its virtue, that whosoever looked upon it should become as stupid as a stone, or like one planet-stricken.

This fable seems to direct the preparation and order that are to be used in making of war : for the more apt and considerate undertaking whereof, three grave and wholesome precepts (savouring of the wisdom of Pallas) are to be observed.

First, that men do not much trouble themselves about the conquest of neighbour nations, seeing that private possessions and empires are enlarged by different means ; for in the augmentation of private revenues the vicinity of men's territories is to be considered, but in the propagation of public dominions, the occasion and facility of making war, and the fruit to be expected, ought to be instead of vicinity. Certainly the Romans, what time their conquests towards the West scarce reached beyond Liguria, did yet in the East bring all the provinces, as far as the mountain Taurus, within the compass of their arms and command ; and therefore Perseus, although he were born and bred in the East, did not yet refuse to undertake an expedition even to the uttermost bounds of the West.

Secondly, there must be a care had that the motives of war be just and honourable : for that begets an alacrity, as well in the soldiers that fight, as in the people that afford pay; it draws on and procures aids, and brings many other commodities besides. But there is no pretence to take up arms more pious than the suppressing of tyranny, under which yoke the people lose their courage, and are cast down without heart and vigour, as in the sight of Medusa.

Thirdly, it is wisely added, that seeing there were three Gorgons by which wars are represented, Perseus undertook her only that was mortal—that is, he made choice of such a kind of war as was likely to be effected and brought to a period, not pursuing vast and endless hopes.

The furnishing of Perseus with necessaries was that which only advanced his attempt, and drew fortune to be of his side, for he had speed from Mercury, concealing of his counsels from Orcus, and providence from Pallas.

Neither is it without an allegory, and that full of matter too, that those wings of celerity were fastened to Perseus' heels, and not to his ankles, to his feet and not to his shoulders; because speed and celerity are required not so much in the first preparations for war, as in those things which second and yield aid to the first; for there is no error in war more frequent than that prosecutions and subsidiary forces do fail to answer the alacrity of the first onsets.

Now for that helmet which Pluto gave him, powerful to make men invisible, the moral is plain: but that twofold gift of providence (to wit, the shield and looking-glass) is full of morality; for that kind of providence which, like a shield, avoids the force of blows, is not alone needful, but that also by which the strength, and motions, and counsels of the enemy are descried, as in the looking-glass of Pallas.

But Perseus, albeit he were sufficiently furnished with aid and courage, yet was he to do one thing of special importance before he entered the lists with this monster, and that was to have some intelligence with the Greæ. These Greæ are treasons, which may be termed the sisters of war, not descended of the same stock, but far unlike in nobility of birth; for wars are general and heroical, but treasons are base and ignoble. Their description is elegant, for they are said to be grey-headed, and like old women from their birth, by reason that traitors are continually vexed with cares and trepidations. But all their strength (before they break out into open rebellions) consists either in an eye or in a tooth; for every faction alienated from any State contemplates and bites. Besides, this eye and tooth are as it were common; for whatsoever they can learn and know is delivered and carried from one to another by the hands of faction. And as concerning the tooth they do all bite alike, and sing the same song, so that hear one and you hear all. Perseus, therefore, was to deal with these Greæ for the love of their eye and tooth. Their eye to discover, their tooth to sow rumours and stir up envy, and to molest and trouble the minds of men. These things therefore being thus disposed and prepared, he addresseth himself to the action of war, and sets upon Medusa as she sleeps : for a wise captain will never assault his enemy when he is unprepared and most secure : and then is there good use of Pallas's glass, for most men, before it come to the push, can acutely pry into and discern their enemies' estate; but the best use of this glass is in the very point of danger, that the manner of it may be so considered, as that the terror may not discourage—which is signified by that looking into this glass with the face turned from Medusa.

The monster's head being cut off, there follow two effects : the first was the procreation and raising of Pegasus, by which may evidently be understood Fame, that, flying through the world, proclaims victory; the second is the bearing of Medusa's head in his shield, to which there is no kind of defence for excellency comparable; for one famous and memorable act prosperously effected and brought to pass, doth restrain the motions and insolences of enemies, and makes Envy herself silent and amazed.

VIII.

ENDYMION, OR A FAVOURITE.

It is said that Luna was in love with the shepherd Endymion, and in a strange and unwonted manner

betrayed her affection; for he, lying in a cave framed
by Nature under the mountain Latmos, she oftentimes
descended from her sphere to enjoy his company as he
slept, and after she had kissed him ascended up
again. Yet notwithstanding this, his idleness and
sleepy security did not any way impair his estate or
fortune; for Luna brought it so to pass, that he alone,
of all the rest of the shepherds, had his flock in best
plight, and most fruitful.

This fable may have reference to the nature and
disposition of princes: for they, being full of doubts
and prone to jealousy, do not easily acquaint men of
prying and curious eyes, and as it were of vigilant and
wakeful dispositions, with the secret humours and
manners of their life, but such rather as are of quiet
and observant natures, suffering them to do what they
list without further scanning, making as if they were
ignorant and perceiving nothing, but of a stupid
disposition and possessed with sleep, yielding unto
them simple obedience, rather than sly compliments;
for it pleaseth princes now and then to descend from
their thrones of majesty, like Luna from the superior
orb, and laying aside their robes of dignity, which
always to be cumbered with would seem a kind of
burden, familiarly to converse with men of this
condition, which they think may be done without
danger; a quality chiefly noted in Tiberius Cæsar,
who, of all others, was a prince most severe; yet such
only were gracious in his favour, as, being well
acquainted with his disposition, did yet constantly

dissemble as if they knew nothing. This was the custom also of Lewis the Eleventh, King of France, a cautious and wily prince.

Neither is it without elegance that the cave of Endymion is mentioned in the fable, because it is a thing usual with such as are the favourites of princes, to have certain pleasant retiring-places whither to invite them for recreation, both of body and mind, and that without hurt or prejudice to their fortunes also. And, indeed, these kind of favourites are men commonly well to pass; for princes, although peradventure they promote them not ever to places of honour, yet do they advance them sufficiently by their favour and countenance; neither do they affect them thus only to serve their own turn, but are wont to enrich them now and then with great dignities and bounties.

IX.

THE SISTER OF THE GIANTS, OR FAME.

It is a poetical relation, that the giants begotten of the Earth made war upon Jupiter and the other gods, and by the force of lightning they were resisted and overthrown. Whereat the Earth, being excited to wrath

in revenge of her children, brought forth Fame, the
youngest sister of the giants.

> "*Illam, terra parens ira irritata Deorum,*
>   *Extremam (ut perhibent) Cœo Enceladoque sororem,*
>   *Progenuit.*"

> "Provoked by wrathful gods, the mother Earth
>   Gives Fame, the giant's youngest sister, birth."

The meaning of the fable seems to be thus :—By the
Earth is signified the nature of the vulgar, always
swollen and malignant, and still broaching new
scandals against superiors, and having gotten fit
opportunity, stirs up rebels, and seditious persons,
that with impious courage do molest princes, and endeavour to subvert their estates, but being suppressed,
the same natural disposition of the people still leaning
to the viler sort, being impatient of peace and tranquillity, spread rumours, raise malicious slanders,
repining whisperings, infamous libels, and others of
that kind, to the detraction of them that are in
authority : so as rebellious actions, and seditious
reports, differ nothing in kind and blood, but as it
were in sex only, the one sort being masculine, the
other feminine.

X.

ACTÆON AND PENTHEUS, OR A CURIOUS MAN.

THE curiosity of men in prying into secrets, and coveting with an indiscreet desire to attain the knowledge of things forbidden, is set forth by the ancients in two examples: the one of Actæon, the other of Pentheus.

Actæon having unawares, and as it were by chance, beheld Diana naked, was turned into a stag, and devoured by his own dogs.

And Pentheus, climbing up into a tree with a desire to be a spectator of the hidden sacrifices of Bacchus, was stricken with such a kind of frenzy, as that whatsoever he looked upon he thought it always double, supposing (among other things) he saw two suns, and two Thebes, insomuch that running towards Thebes, spying another Thebes, instantly turned back again, and so kept still running forward and backward with perpetual unrest.

"*Eumenidum veluti demens videt agmina Pentheus,*
  Et solem geminum, et duplices se ostendere Thebas."

"Pentheus amazed doth troops of furies spy,
  And sun and Thebes seem double to his eye."

The first of the fables pertains to the secrets of

princes, the second to divine mysteries. For those
that are near about princes, and come to the knowledge
of more secrets than they would have them, do certainly
incur great hatred, and therefore, suspecting that
they are shot at, and opportunities watched for their
overthrow, do lead their lives like stags, fearful and
full of suspicion. And it happens oftentimes that
their servants, and those of their household, to insinuate
into the prince's favour, do accuse them to their
destruction; for against whomsoever the prince's displeasure is known, look how many servants that man
hath, and you shall find them for the most part so
many traitors unto him, that his end may prove to be
like Actæon's.

The other is the misery of Pentheus, for they that, by
the height of knowledge in nature and philosophy,
having climbed, as it were, into a tree, do with rash
attempts (unmindful of their frailty) pry into the
secrets of Divine mysteries, are justly plagued
with perpetual inconstancy, and with wavering and
perplexed conceits: for seeing the light of Nature is
one thing, and of Grace another, it happens so to them
as if they saw two suns. And seeing the actions of
life and decrees of will do depend on the understanding,
it follows that they doubt, and are inconstant, no less
in will than in opinion, and so in like manner they may
be said to see two Thebes; for by Thebes, seeing there
was the habitation and refuge of Pentheus, is meant
the end of actions. Hence it comes to pass that they
know not whither they go, but, as distracted and

unresolved in the scope of their intentions, are in all things carried about with sudden passions of the mind.

XI.

ORPHEUS, OR PHILOSOPHY.

THE tale of Orpheus, though common, had never the fortune to be fitly applied in every point. It may seem to represent the image of philosophy; for the person of Orpheus (a man admirable and divine, and so excellently skilled in all kind of harmony, that with his sweet ravishing music he did as it were charm and allure all things to follow him) may carry a singular description of philosophy: for the labours of Orpheus do so far exceed the labours of Hercules in dignity and efficacy, as the works of wisdom excel the works of fortitude.

Orpheus, for the love he bare to his wife (snatched, as it were, from him by untimely death), resolved to go down to hell with his harp, to try if he might obtain her of the infernal powers. Neither were his hopes frustrated: for having appeased them with the melodious sound of his voice and touch, he prevailed at length so far as that they granted him leave to take her away with him, but on this condition, that she should follow him, and he should not look back upon her till he came to the light of the upper world; which he impatient of, out of love and care, and thinking that he was in a manner past all danger, nevertheless violated, insomuch that the covenant was broken, and she forthwith tumbled back again headlong into hell. From that time Orpheus, falling into a deep melancholy, became a contemner of womenkind, and bequeathed himself to a solitary life in the deserts, where, by the same melody of his voice and harp, he first drew all manner of wild beasts unto him, who, forgetful of their savage fierceness, and casting off the precipitate provocations of lust and fury, not caring to satiate their voracity by hunting after prey, as at a theatre, in fawning and reconciled amity one towards another, stand all at the gaze about him, and attentively lend their ears to his music. Neither is this all: for so great was the power and alluring force of his harmony, that he drew the woods, and moved the very stones to come and place themselves in an orderly and decent fashion about him. These things succeeding happily and with great admiration for a time, at length certain Thracian women, possessed with the spirit of Bacchus, made such a horrid and strange noise with their cornets, that the sound of Orpheus's harp could no more be heard, insomuch as that harmony, which was the bond of that order and society, being dissolved, all disorder began again, and the beasts, returning to their wonted nature, pursued one another unto death as before: neither did the trees or stones remain any longer in their places;

and Orpheus himself was by these female furies torn in pieces and scattered all over the desert; for whose cruel death the river Helicon, sacred to the Muses, in horrible indignation hid his head underground, and raised it again in another place.

The meaning of this fable seems to be thus:— Orpheus's music is of two sorts, the one appeasing the infernal powers, the other attracting beasts and trees. The first may be fitly applied to natural philosophy, the second to moral or civil discipline.

The most noble work of natural philosophy is the restitution and renovation of things corruptible; the other, as a lesser degree of it, the preservation of bodies in their estate, detaining them from dissolution and putrefaction. And if this gift may be in mortals, certainly it can be done by no other means than by the due and exquisite temper of nature, as by the melody and delicate touch of an instrument. But seeing it is of all things the most difficult, it is seldom or never attained unto, and in all likelihood for no other reason more than through curious diligence and untimely impatience. And therefore philosophy, hardly able to produce so excellent an effect, in a pensive humour (and not without cause) busies herself about human objects, and by persuasion and eloquence, insinuating the love of virtue, equity, and concord in the minds of men, draws multitudes of people to a society, makes them subject to laws, obedient to government, and forgetful of their unbridled affections, whilst they give ear to precepts, and submit themselves to discipline, whence follows the building of houses, erecting of towns, and planting of fields and orchards with trees and the like, insomuch that it would not be amiss to say that even thereby stones and woods were called together and settled in order. And after serious trial made and frustrated about the restoring of a body mortal, this care of civil affairs follows in its due place, because, by a plain demonstration of the inevitable necessity of death, men's minds are moved to seek eternity by the fame and glory of their merits. It is wisely, also, said in the fable that Orpheus was averse from the love of women and marriage, because the delights of wedlock and love of children do for the most part hinder men from enterprising great and noble designs for the public good, holding posterity a sufficient step to immortality, without actions.

Besides, even the very works of wisdom, although amongst all human things they do most excel, do nevertheless meet with their periods. For it happens that after kingdoms and commonwealths have flourished for a time, even tumults, and seditions, and wars arise; in the midst of which hurly-burlies, first, laws are silent, men return to the pravity of their natures, fields and towns are wasted and depopulated; and then, if this fury continue, learning and philosophy must needs be dismembered, so that a few fragments only, and in some places, will be found, like the scattered boards of shipwreck, so as a barbarous age must follow; and the streams of Helicon are hid under the earth until, the vicissitude of things passing, they break out again and appear in some other remote nation, though not, perhaps, in the same climate.

XII.

CŒLUM, OR BEGINNINGS.

WE have it from the poets by tradition that Cœlum was the ancientest of the gods, and that his members of generation were cut off by his son Saturn. Saturn had many children, but devoured them as soon as they were born. Jupiter only escaped, who, being come to man's estate, thrust Saturn, his father, into hell, and so usurped the kingdom. Moreover, he dismembered his father with the same falchion that Saturn dismembered Cœlum, and cast what he struck off into the sea, from whence came Venus. Not long after this, Jupiter, being scarce settled and confirmed in this kingdom, was invaded by two memorable wars. The first was of the Titans, in the suppressing of which Sol, who alone of all the Titans favoured Jupiter's side, took exceeding great pains. The second was of the giants, whom Jupiter himself destroyed with thunderbolts, and so, all wars being ended, he reigned secure.

This fable seems enigmatically to show from whence

all things took their beginning, not much differing from that opinion of philosophers, which Democritus afterwards laboured to maintain, attributing eternity to the first matter and not to the world; in which he comes somewhat near the truth of Divine Writ, telling us of a huge deformed mass before the beginning of the six days' work.

The meaning of the fable is this: By Cœlum may be understood that vast concavity, or vaulted compass, that comprehends all matter; and by Saturn may be meant the matter itself, which takes from its parent all power of generating; for the universality, or whole bulk of matter always remains the same, neither increasing nor diminishing in respect of the quality of its nature. But by the divers agitations and motions of it, were first produced imperfect and ill-agreeing compositions of things, making, as it were, certain worlds for proofs or assays, and so in process of time a perfect fabric or structure was framed, which should still retain and keep his form. And therefore the government of the first age was shadowed by the kingdom of Saturn, who, for the frequent dissolutions and short continuances of things, was aptly feigned to devour his children. The succeeding government was deciphered by the reign of Jupiter, who confined those continual mutations unto Tartarus, a place signifying perturbation. This place seems to be all that middle space between the lower superficies of heaven and the centre of the earth, in which all perturbation and fragility and mortality or corruption are frequent.

During the former generation of things, in the time of Saturn's reign, Venus was not born; for so long as in the universality of matter discord was better and more prevalent than concord, it was necessary that there should be a total dissolution or mutation, and that in the whole fabric. And by this kind of generation were creatures produced before Saturn was deprived of his members. When this ceased, that other which is wrought by Venus immediately came in; consisting in settled and prevalent concord of things, so that mutation should be only in respect of the parts, the universal fabric remaining whole and inviolate.

Saturn, they say, was deposed and cast down into hell, but not destroyed and utterly extinguished, because there was an opinion that the world should relapse into the old chaos and interregnum again, which Lucretius prayed might not happen in his time.

> " *Quod procul à nobis, flectat fortuna gubernans*
> *Et ratio potius, quam res persuadeat ipsa.*"

> "Oh, guiding Providence, be gracious,
> That this doomsday be far removed from us;
> And grant that by us it may be expected,
> Rather than on us in our times effected."

For afterwards the world should subsist by its own quantity and power. Yet from the beginning there was no rest: for in the celestial regions there first followed notable mutations, which, by the power of the sun, predominating over superior bodies, were so quieted, that the state of the world should be conserved; and afterwards, in inferior bodies, by the suppressing and dissipating of inundations, tempests, winds, and general earthquakes, a more peaceful and durable agreement and tranquillity of things followed. But of this fable it may convertibly be said that the fable contains philosophy, and philosophy, again, the fable; for we know by faith that all these things are nothing else but the long-since ceasing and failing oracles of sense, seeing that both the matter and fabric of the world are most truly referred to a Creator.

XIII.

PROTEUS, OR MATTER.

THE poets say that Proteus was Neptune's herdman, a grave sire, and so excellent a prophet that he might well be termed thrice excellent; for he knew not only things to come, but even things past, as well as present, so that besides his skill in divination he was the messenger and interpreter of all antiquities and hidden mysteries. The place of his abode was a huge, vast cave, where his custom was every day at noon to count his flock of sea-calves, and then to go to sleep. Moreover, he that desired his advice in anything could by no other means obtain it but by catching him in manacles, and holding him fast therewith; who, nevertheless, to be at liberty would turn himself into all manner of forms and wonders of nature—sometimes into fire, sometimes into water, sometimes into the shape of beasts and the like, till at length he was restored to his own form again.

This fable may seem to unfold the secrets of nature and the properties of matter. For under the person of Proteus the first matter (which, next to God, is the ancientest thing) may be represented; for matter dwells in the concavity of heaven as in a cave.

He is Neptune's bondman because the operations and dispensations of matter are chiefly exercised in liquid bodies.

His flock or herd seems to be nothing but the ordinary species of sensible creatures, plants, and metals, in which Matter seems to diffuse and, as it were, spend itself, so that after the forming and perfecting of these kinds (having ended, as it were, her task), she seems to sleep and take her rest, not attempting the composition of any more species. And this may be the moral of Proteus's counting his flock, and of his sleeping.

Now this is said to be done, not in the morning, nor in the evening, but at noon; to wit, at such time as is most fit and convenient for the perfecting and bringing forth of species out of matter, duly prepared and predisposed, and in the middle, as it were, between their beginnings and declinations, which we know sufficiently (out of the holy history), to be done about the time of the creation; for then, by the power of that divine word *Producat*, matter at the Creator's command did congregate itself, not by ambages nor turnings, but instantly, to the production of its work into act and the constitution of species. And thus far have we the narration of Proteus, free and unrestrained, together with his flock complete; for the universality of things, with their ordinary structures and compositions of species, bears the face of matter not limited and constrained, and of the flock also of material beings. Nevertheless, if any expert minister of nature shall encounter matter by main force, vexing, and urging her, with intent and purpose to reduce her to nothing, she contrarywise, seeing annihilation and absolute destruction cannot be effected but by the omnipotency of God, being thus caught in the straits of necessity, doth change and turn herself into divers strange forms and shapes of things, so that at length, by fetching a circuit, as it were, she comes to a period, and if the force continue, betakes herself to her former being; the reason of which constraint or binding will be more facile and expedite if matter be laid hold on by manacles, that is, by extremities.

Now, whereas it is feigned that Proteus was a prophet, well skilled in three differences of times, it hath an excellent agreement with the nature of matter; for it is necessary that he that will know the properties and proceedings of matter should comprehend in his understanding the sum of all things, which have

c—15

been, which are, or which shall be, although no knowledge can extend so far as to singular and individual beings.

XIV.

MEMNON, OR A YOUTH TOO FORWARD.

THE poets say that Memnon was the son of Aurora, who, adorned with beautiful armour, and animated with popular applause, came to the Trojan war, where in a rash boldness, hasting unto and thirsting after glory, he entered into single combat with Achilles, the valiantest of all the Grecians, by whose powerful hand he was there slain. But Jupiter, pitying his destruction, sent birds to modulate certain lamentable and doleful notes at the solemnisation of his funeral obsequies; whose statue also, the sun reflecting on it with his morning beams, did usually, as is reported, send forth a mournful sound.

This fable may be applied to the unfortunate destinies of hopeful young men, who, like the son of Aurora, puffed up with the glittering show of vanity and ostentation, attempt actions above their strength, and provoke and press the most valiant heroes to combat with them, so that, meeting with their over-match, they are vanquished and destroyed, and their untimely death is oft accompanied with much pity and commiseration. For among all the disasters that can happen to mortals, there is none so lamentable and so powerful to move compassion as the flower of virtue cropped with too sudden a mischance. Neither hath it been often known that men in their green years become so loathsome and odious as that at their deaths either sorrow is stinted or commiseration moderated. But that lamentation and mourning do not only flutter about their obsequies like those funeral birds, but this pitiful commiseration doth continue for a long space, and especially by occasions and new motions, and beginning of great matters, as it were by the morning rays of the sun, their passions and desires are renewed.

XV.

TITHONUS, OR SATIETY.

IT is elegantly feigned that Tithonus was the paramour of Aurora, who, desirous for ever to enjoy his company, petitioned Jupiter that he might never die, but through womanish oversight forgetting to insert this clause in her petition, that he might not withal grow old and feeble, it followed that he was only freed from the condition of mortality. But old age came upon him in a marvellous and miserable fashion, agreeable to the state of those who cannot die yet every day grow weaker and weaker with age. Insomuch that Jupiter, in commiseration of this his misery, did at length metamorphose him into a grasshopper.

This fable seems to be an ingenuous character or description of pleasure, which in the beginning, and, as it were, in the morning, seems to be so pleasant and delightful, that men desire they might enjoy and monopolise it for ever unto themselves, unmindful of that satiety and loathing, which, like old age, will come upon them before they be aware. And so at last when the use of pleasure leaves men, the desire and affection not yet yielding unto death, it comes to pass that men please themselves only by talking and commemorating those things which brought pleasure unto them in the flower of their age, which may be observed in libidinous persons, and also in men of military professions—the one delighting in beastly talk, the other boasting of their valorous deeds, like grasshoppers, whose vigour consists only in their voice.

XVI.

JUNO'S SUITOR, OR BASENESS.

THE poets say that Jupiter, to enjoy his amorous delights, took upon him the shape of sundry creatures, as of a bull, of an eagle, of a swan, and of a golden shower; but being a suitor to Juno, he came in a form most ignoble and base, an object full of contempt and scorn, resembling, indeed, a miserable cuckoo, weather-beaten with rain and tempest, numbed, quaking, and half dead with cold.

This fable is wise, and seems to be taken out of the bowels of morality, the sense of it being this :—That men boast not too much of themselves, thinking by ostentation of their own worth to insinuate themselves into estimation and favour with men, the success of such intentions being for the most part measured by the nature and disposition of those to whom men sue for grace, who, if of themselves they be endowed with no gifts and ornaments of nature, but are only of haughty and malignant spirits (intimated by the person of Juno), then are suitors to know that it is good policy to omit all kind of appearance that may any way show their own least praise or worth, and that they much deceive themselves in taking any other course. Neither is it enough to show deformity in obsequiousness, unless they also appear even abject and base in their very persons.

XVII.

CUPID, OR AN ATOM.

THAT which the poets say of Cupid or Love cannot properly be attributed to one and the self-same person; and yet the difference is such, that, by rejecting the confusion of persons, the similitude may be received.

They say that Love is the ancientest of all the gods, and of all things else except Chaos, which they hold to be a contemporary with it. Now, as touching Chaos, that by the ancients was never dignified with divine honour, or with the title of a god. And as for Love, they absolutely bring him in without a father, only some are of opinion that he came of an egg which was laid by Nox, and that of Chaos he begot the gods and all things else. There are four things attributed unto him—perpetual infancy, blindness, nakedness, and an archery. There was also another Love, which was the youngest of the gods, and he, they say, was the son of Venus. On this also they bestow the attributes of the elder Love, as in some sort well applied unto him.

This fable tends and looks to the cradle of Nature, Love seeming to be the appetite or desire of the first matter, or (to speak more plain) the natural motion of the atom, which is that ancient and only power that forms and fashions all things out of matter of which

there is no parent—that is to say, no cause, seeing
every cause is as a parent to its effect. Of this power
or virtue there can be no cause in Nature (as for God,
we always except Him), for nothing was before it, and
therefore no efficient cause of it. Neither was there
anything better known to Nature, and therefore neither
genus nor form. Wherefore, whatsoever it is, positive
it is, and but inexpressible. Moreover, if the manner
and proceeding of it were to be conceived, yet could it
not be any cause, seeing that (next unto God) it is the
cause of causes, itself only without any cause. And
perchance there is no likelihood that the manner of it
may be contained or comprehended within the narrow
compass of human search. Not without reason, therefore, is it feigned to come of an egg which was laid
by Nox. Certainly the divine philosopher grants so
much (Eccl. iii. 11): " *Cuncta fecit tempestatibus suis
pulchra, et mundum tradidit disputationibus eorum,
ita tamen ut non inveniat homo opus quod operatus
est deus, à principio ad finem.*" That is, He hath made
everything beautiful in their seasons, also He hath set
the world in their meditations, yet cannot man find
out the work that God hath wrought from the beginning even to the end. For the principal law of
nature, or power of this desire, created by God in
these parcels of things, for concurring and meeting
together (from whose repetitions and multiplications
all variety of creatures proceeded and were composed),
may dazzle the eye of men's understandings, and comprehended it can hardly be. The Greek philosophers

are observed to be very acute and diligent in searching out the material principles of things; but in the beginnings of motion, wherein consists all the efficacy of operation, they are negligent and weak, and in this that we handle they seem to be altogether blind and stammering; for the opinion of the Peripatics concerning the appetite of matter caused by privation is in a manner nothing else but words, which rather sound than signify any reality. And those that refer it unto God do very well; but then they leap up, they ascend not by degrees; for doubtless there is one chief law subordinate to God, in which all natural things concur and meet; the same that in the fore-cited Scripture is demonstrated in these words: "*Opus, quod operatus est Deus à principio usque ad finem*"—"The work that God hath wrought from the beginning even to the end." But Democritus, who entered more deeply into the consideration of this point, after he had conceived an atom with some small dimension and form, he attributed unto it only one desire, or first motion simply or absolutely, and another comparatively or in respect; for he thought that all things did properly tend to the centre of the world, whereof those bodies which were more material descended with swifter motion, and those that had less matter did, on the contrary, tend upward. But this meditation was very shallow, containing less than was expedient; for neither the turning of the celestial bodies in a round, nor shutting and opening of things, may seem to be reduced or applied to this beginning. And as for that opinion of Epicurus concerning the casual declination and agitation of the atom, it is but a mere toy, and a plain evidence that he was ignorant of that point. It is therefore more apparent than we could wish that this Cupid or Love remains as yet clouded under the shades of night. Now, as concerning his attributes: he is elegantly described with perpetual infancy or childhood, because compound bodies they seem greater and more stricken in years; whereas the first seeds of things or atoms, they are little and diminute, and always in their infancy.

He is also well feigned to be naked, because all compound bodies to a man rightly judging seem to be apparelled and clothed, and nothing to be properly naked but the first particles of things.

Concerning his blindness, the allegory is full of wisdom; for this Love or desire (whatsoever it may be) seems to have but little providence, as directing his pace and motion by that which it perceives nearest, not unlike blind men that go by feeling. More admirable, then, must that chief divine providence be, which from things empty and destitute of providence, and, as it were, blind, by a constant and fatal law, produceth so excellent an order and beauty of things.

The last thing which is attributed unto Love is archery, by which is meant that his virtue is such as that it works upon a distant object, because that whatsoever operates afar off seems to shoot, as it were, an arrow. Wherefore whosoever holds the being both of atoms and vacuity must needs infer that the virtue of the atom reacheth to a distant object; for if it were not so, there could be no motion at all, by reason of the interposition of vacuity, but all things would stand stone still, and remain immovable.

Now, as touching that other Cupid or Love, he may well be termed the youngest of the gods, because he could have no being before the constitution of species; and in his description the allegory may be applied and traduced to manners. Nevertheless, he holds some kind of conformity with the elder; for Venus doth generally stir up a desire, and Cupid, her son, doth apply this desire to some individual nature, so that the general disposition comes from Venus, the more exact sympathy from Cupid—the one derived from causes more near, the other from beginnings more remote and fatal, and, as it were, from the elder Cupid, of whom every exquisite sympathy doth depend.

XVIII.

DIOMEDES, OR ZEAL.

DIOMEDES, flourishing with great fame and glory in the Trojan wars, and in high favour with Pallas, was by her instigated (being, indeed, forwarder than he should have been) not to forbear Venus a jot, if he encountered with her in fight, which very boldly he did, wounding her in the right arm. This presumptuous fact he carried clear for a while, and, being honoured and renowned for his many heroic deeds, at last returned into his own country, where, finding himself hard bested with domestic troubles, he fled into Italy, betaking himself to the protection of foreigners. There, in the beginning, he was fortunate, and royally entertained by King Daunus with sumptuous gifts, and honoured with many statues throughout his dominions; but upon the very first calamity that happened unto this nation whereunto he was fled for succour, King Daunus enters into a conceit with himself that he had entertained a wicked guest into his family, and a man odious to the gods, and an impugner of their divinity, who had dared with his sword to assault and wound that goddess, whom in their religion they held it sacrilege so much as to touch. Therefore, that he might expiate his country's guilt (nothing respecting the duties of hospitality, when the bonds of religion tied him with a more reverend regard), suddenly he slew Diomedes, commanding withal that his trophies and statues should be abolished and destroyed. Neither was it safe to lament this miserable destiny; but even his companions in arms, whilst they mourned at the funeral of their captain, and filled all the places with plaints and lamentations, were suddenly metamorphosed into birds like unto swans, who, when their death approacheth, sing melodious and mournful hymns.

This fable hath a most rare and singular subject; for in any of the poetical records, wherein the heroes are mentioned, we find not that any one of them, besides Diomedes, did ever with his sword offer violence to any of the deities. And, indeed, the fable seems in him to represent the nature and fortune of man, who of himself doth propound and make this as the end of all his actions, to worship some divine power, or to follow some sect of religion, though never so vain and superstitious, and with force and arms to defend the same; for although those bloody quarrels for religion were unknown to the ancients (the heathen gods not having so much as a touch of that jealousy which is an attribute of the true God), yet the wisdom of the ancient times seems to be so copious and full, as that what was not known by experience was yet comprehended by meditation and fictions. They, then, that endeavour to reform and convince any sect of religion (though vain, corrupt, and infamous, shadowed by the person of Venus), not by the force of argument, and doctrine, and holiness of life, and by the weight of examples and authority, but labour to extirpate and root it out by fire and sword and tortures, are encouraged, it may be, thereunto by Pallas—that is, by the acrity of prudence and severity of judgment, by whose vigour and efficacy they see into the falsity and vanity of these errors. And by this their hatred of pravity, and good zeal to religion, they purchase to themselves great glory, and by the vulgar (to whom nothing moderate can be grateful) are esteemed and honoured as the only supporters of truth and religion, when others seem to be lukewarm, and full of fear. Yet this glory and happiness doth seldom endure to the end, seeing every violent prosperity, if it prevent not alteration by an untimely death, grows to be so unprosperous at last; for if it happen that by a change of government this banished and depressed sect get strength, and so bear up again, then these zealous men, so fierce in opposition before, are condemned, their very names are hateful, and all their glory ends in obloquy.

In that Diomedes is said to be murdered by his host; it gives us to understand that the difference of religion breeds deceit and treachery, even among nearest acquaintance.

Now in that lamentation and mourning was not tolerated, but punished: it puts us in mind that, let there be never so nefarious an act done, yet there is some place left for commiseration and pity—that even those that hate offences should yet in humanity commiserate offenders and pity their distress, it being the extremity of evil when mercy is not suffered to have commerce with misery. Yea, even in the cause as well of religion as impiety, many men may be noted and observed to have been compassionate. But, on the contrary, the complaints and moans of Diomedes' followers—that is, of men of the same sect and opinion—are won to be shrill and loud, like swans, or the birds of Diomedes. In whom also that part of the allegory is excellent, to signify that the last words of those that suffer death for religion, like the songs of dying swans, do wonderfully work upon the minds of men, and stick and remain a long time in their senses and memories.

XIX.

DÆDALUS, OR MECHANIC.

MECHANICAL wisdom and industry, and in it unlawful science perverted to wrong ends, is shadowed by the ancients under the person of Dædalus, a man ingenious, but execrable. This Dædalus, for murdering his fellow-servant that emulated him, being banished, was kindly entertained during his exile in many cities and princes' courts; for, indeed, he was the raiser and builder of many goodly structures, as well in honour of the gods as for the beauty and magnificence of cities and other public places; but for his works of mischief he is most notorious. It is he which framed that engine which Pasiphæ used, to satisfy herself in companying with a bull, so that by this his wretched industry and pernicious device, that monster Minotaur (the destruction of so many hopeful youths) took his accursed and infamous beginning; and, studying to cover and increase one mischief with another, for the security and preservation of this monster he invented and built a labyrinth, a work for intent and use most nefarious and wicked, for skill and workmanship famous and excellent. Afterward, that he might not be noted only for works of mischief, but be sought after as well for remedies as for instruments of destruction, he was the author of that ingenious device concerning the clue of thread, by which the labyrinth was made passable without any let. This Dædalus was persecuted by Minos with great severity, diligence, and inquiry, but he always found the means to avoid and escape his tyranny. Lastly, he taught his son Icarus to fly, but the novice, in ostentation of his art, soaring too high, fell into the sea, and was drowned.

The parable seems to be thus: In the beginning of it may be noted that kind of envy or emulation that lodgeth, and wonderfully sways and domineers, amongst excellent artificers, there being no kind of people more reciprocally tormented with bitter and deadly hatred than they.

The banishment, also, of Dædalus (a punishment inflicted on him against the rules of policy and providence) is worth the noting: for artificers have this prerogative to find entertainment and welcome in all countries, so that exile to an excellent workman can hardly be termed a punishment, whereas other conditions and states of life can scarce live out of their own country. The admiration of artificers is propagated and increased in foreign and strange nations, seeing it is a natural and inbred disposition of men to value their own countrymen in respect of mechanical work less than strangers.

Concerning the use of mechanical arts, that which follows is plain. The life of man is much beholding to them, seeing many things conducing to the ornament of religion, to the grace of civil discipline, and to the beautifying of all human-kind, are extracted out of their treasuries; and yet, notwithstanding, from the same magazine or storehouse are produced instruments both of lust and death, for we well know how far exquisite poisons, warlike engines, and such-like mischiefs (the effects of mechanical inventions), do exceed the Minotaur himself in malignity and savage cruelty.

Moreover, that of the labyrinth is an excellent allegory, whereby is shadowed the nature of mechanical sciences, for all such handicraft works as are more ingenious and accurate may be compared to a labyrinth in respect of subtilty and divers intricate passages, and in other plain resemblances, which by the eye of judgment can hardly be guided and discerned, but only by the line of experience.

Neither is it impertinently added that he which invented the intricate nooks of the labyrinth did also show the commodity of the clue; for mechanical arts are of ambiguous use, serving as well for hurt as for remedy, and they have, in a manner, power both to loose and bind themselves.

Unlawful trades, and so by consequence arts themselves, are often persecuted by Minos—that is, by laws, which do condemn them and prohibit men to use them. Nevertheless, they are hid and retained everywhere, finding lurking holes and places of receipt, which was well observed by Tacitus of the mathematicians and figure-flingers of his time in a thing not much unlike: "*Genus (inquit) hominum quod in civitate nostra semper et retinebitur et vetabitur*"— "There is a kind of men (saith he) that will always abide in our city, though always forbidden." And yet, notwithstanding, unlawful and curious arts of what kind soever, in tract of time, when they cannot perform what they promise, do fall from the good opinion that was held of them (no otherwise than as Icarus fell down from the skies), they grow to be contemned and scorned, and so perish by too much ostentation. And, to say the truth, they are not so happily restrained by the reins of law, as bewrayed by their own vanity.

XX.

ERICTHONIUS, OR IMPOSTURE.

THE poets fable that Vulcan solicited Minerva for her love, and, impatient of denial, with an inflamed desire offered her violence; but in struggling his seed fell upon the ground, whereof came Ericthonius, whose body from the middle upward was of a comely and apt proportion, but his thighs and legs like the tail of an eel, small and deformed; he, being conscious of this monstrosity, became the first inventor of the use of chariots, whereby that part of his body which was well proportioned might be seen, and the other, which was ugly and uncomely, might be hid.

This strange and prodigious fiction may seem to show that art (which for the great use it hath of fire is shadowed by Vulcan), although it labour by much striving with corporeal substances to force Nature, and to make her subject to it (she being for her industrious works rightly represented by Minerva), yet seldom or never attains the end it aims at, but with much ado and great pains, wrestling, as it were, with her, comes short of its purpose, and produceth certain imperfect births and lame works, fair to the eye, but weak and defective in use, which many impostors with much subtilty and deceit set to view, and carry about as it were in triumph: as may for the most part be noted in chemical productions and other mechanical subtilties and novelties, especially when, rather prosecuting their intent than reclining their errors, they rather strive to overcome nature by force than sue for her embracements by due obsequiousness and observance.

XXI.

DEUCALION, OR RESTITUTION.

THE poets say that the people of the old world being destroyed by a general deluge, Deucalion and Pirrha were only left alive, who, praying with fervent and zealous devotion that they might know by what means to repair mankind, had answer from an oracle that they should obtain what they desired, if, taking the bones of their mother, they cast them behind their backs, which at first struck them with great amazement and despair, seeing (all things being defaced by the flood) it would be an endless work to find their mother's sepulchre; but at length they understood that by bones the stones of the earth (seeing the earth was the mother of all things) were signified by the oracle.

This fable seems to reveal a secret of nature, and to correct an error familiar to men's conceits: for, through want of knowledge, men think that things may take renovation and restoration from their putrefaction and dregs, no otherwise than the Phœnix from the ashes, which in no case can be admitted, seeing such kind of materials, when they have fulfilled their periods, are unapt for the beginnings of such things; we must therefore look back to more common principles.

XXII.

NEMESIS, OR THE VICISSITUDE OF THINGS.

NEMESIS is said to be a goddess venerable unto all, but to be feared of none but potentates and fortune's favourites. She is thought to be the daughter of Oceanus and Nox. She is portrayed with wings on her shoulders, and on her head a coronet, bearing in her right hand a javelin of ash, and in her left a pitcher with the similitudes of Ethiopians engraven on it, and, lastly, she is described sitting on a hart.

The parable may be thus unfolded: Her name Nemesis doth plainly signify revenge or retribution, her office and administration being (like a tribune of the people) to hinder the constant and perpetual felicity of happy men, and to interpose her word, "*Veto*"—

"I forbid the continuance of it"—that is, not only to chastise insolency, but to intermix prosperity, though harmless and in a mean, with the vicissitudes of adversity, as if it were a custom that no mortal man should be admitted to the table of the gods but for sport. Truly, when I read that chapter wherein Caius Plinius hath collected the misfortunes and miseries of Augustus Cæsar, whom of all men I thought the most happy, who had also a kind of art to use and enjoy his fortune, and in whose mind might be noted neither pride, nor lightness, nor niceness, nor disorder, nor melancholy (as that he had appointed a time to die of his own accord), I then deemed this goddess to be great and powerful, to whose altar so worthy a sacrifice as this was drawn.

The parents of this goddess were Oceanus and Nox —that is, the vicissitude of things, and divine judgment obscure and secret; for the alterations of things are aptly represented by the sea, in respect of the continual ebbing and flowing of it; and hidden providence is well set forth by the night, for even the nocturnal Nemesis (seeing human judgment differs much from divine) was seriously observed by the heathen.

Virgil Æneid. Lib. 2.

"————Cadit et Ripheus justissimus unus,
Qui fuit ex Teucris, et servantissimus æqui,
Diis aliter visum."

"That day by Greekish force was Ripheus slain,
So just and strict observer of the law,

As Troy within her walls did not contain
    A better man : yet God then good it saw."

She is described with wings, because the changes of things are so sudden, as that they are seen before fore-seen; for in the records of all ages, we find it for the most part true, that great potentates and wise men have perished by those misfortunes which they most contemned, as may be observed in Marcus Cicero, who, being admonished by Decius Brutus of Octavius Cæsar's hypocritical friendship and hollow-heartedness towards him, returns this answer: "*Te autem, mi Brute, sicut debeo, amo, quod istud quicquid est nugarum me scire voluisti*"—"I must ever acknow-ledge myself, dear Brutus, beholding to thee in love, for that thou hast been so careful to acquaint me with that which I esteem but as a needless trifle to be doubted."

Nemesis is also adorned with a coronet, to show the envious and malignant disposition of the vulgar; for when fortune's favourites and great potentates come to ruin, then do the common people rejoice, setting as it were a crown upon the head of revenge.

The javelin in her right hand points at those, whom she actually strikes and pierceth through.

And before those whom she destroys not in their calamity and misfortune, she ever presents that black and dismal spectacle in her left hand ; for questionless to men sitting, as it were, upon the pinnacle of pros-perity, the thoughts of death, and painfulness of sickness and misfortunes, perfidiousness of friends, treachery of foes, change of state, and such like, seem as ugly to the eye of their meditations as those Ethiopians pictured in Nemesis her pitcher. Virgil, in describing the battle of Actium, speaks thus elegantly of our Cleopatra :—

> *Regina in mediis patrio vocat agmina sistro,*
> *Necdum etiam geminos à tergo respicit angues.*"

> "The Queen amidst this hurly burly stands,
> And with her country timbrel calls her bands ;
> Not spying yet where crawled behind her back
> Two deadly snakes with venom speckled black."

But not long after, which way soever she turned, troops of Ethiopians were still before her eyes.

Lastly, it is wisely added, that Nemesis rides upon an hart, because a hart is a most lively creature. And albeit it may be, that such as are cut off by death in their youth prevent and shun the power of Nemesis, yet doubtless such whose prosperity and power continue long are subject unto her, and lie, as it were, trodden under her feet.

XXIII.

ACHELOUS, OR BATTLE.

IT is a fable of antiquity that when Hercules and Achelous as rivals contended for the marriage of Deianira, the matter drew them to combat, wherein Achelous took upon him many divers shapes, for so was it in his power to do, and amongst others transforming himself into the likeness of a furious wild bull, assaulted Hercules and provoked him to fight. But Hercules for all this, sticking to his old humane form, courageously encounters him, and so the combat goes roundly on. But this was the event, that Hercules tore away one of the bull's horns, wherewith he being mightily daunted and grieved to ransom his horn again, was contented to give Hercules, in exchange thereof, the Amalthean horn, or Cornucopia.

This fable hath relation unto the expeditions of war, for the preparation thereof on the defensive part which (expressed in the person of Achelous) is very diverse and uncertain. But the invading party is most commonly of one sort, and that very single, consisting of an army by land, or perhaps of a navy by sea. But for a king that in his own territory expects an enemy, his occasions are infinite. He fortifies towns, he assembles men out of the countries and villages, he raiseth citadels, he builds and breaks down bridges, he disposeth garrisons, and placeth troops of soldiers on passages of rivers, on ports, on mountains, and ambushes in woods, and is busied with a multitude of other directions, insomuch that every day he prescribeth new forms and orders, and then at last, having accommodated all things complete for defence, he then rightly represents the form and manner of a fierce fighting bull. On the other side, the invader's greatest care is the fear to be distressed for victuals in an enemy's country, and therefore he affects chiefly to hasten on battle; for if it should happen that after a field fought he prove the victor, and, as it were, break the horns of the enemy, then certainly this follows, that his enemy, being stricken with terror and abased in his reputation, presently betrays his weakness, and seeking to repair his loss, retires himself to some stronghold, abandoning to the conqueror the spoil and sack of his country and cities; which may well be termed a type of the Amalthean horn.

XXIV.

DIONYSUS, OR PASSIONS.

THEY say that Semele, Jupiter's sweetheart, having bound her paramour by an irrevocable oath to grant her one request which she would require, desired that he would accompany her in the same form wherein he accompanied Juno; which he granting (as not able to deny), it came to pass that the miserable wench was burnt with lightning. But the infant which she bare in her womb, Jupiter the father took out and kept it in a gash he cut in his thigh till the months were complete that it should be born. This burden made Jupiter somewhat to limp, whereupon the child (because it was heavy and troublesome to its father while it lay in his thigh) was called Dionysus. Being born, it was committed to Proserpina for some years to be nursed, and being grown up, it had such a maiden face as that a man could hardly judge whether it were a boy or a girl. He was dead also, and buried for a time, but afterwards revived. Being but a youth he invented and taught the planting and dressing of vines, the making also and use of wine, for which, becoming famous and renowned; he subjugated the world, even to the uttermost bounds of India. He rode in a chariot drawn with tigers. There danced about him certain deformed goblins called Cobali, Acratus, and others, yea, even the Muses also were some of his followers. He took to wife Ariadne, forsaken and left by Theseus. The tree sacred unto him was the Ivy. He was held the inventor and institutor of sacrifices and ceremonies, and full of corruption and cruelty. He had power to strike men with fury or madness; for it is reported that at the celebration of his orgies, two famous worthies. Pentheus and Orpheus, were torn in pieces by certain frantic women, the one because he got upon a tree to behold their ceremonies in these sacrifices, the other for making melody with his harp. And for his guests they are in a manner the same with Jupiter's.

There is such excellent morality couched in this fable, as that " Moral Philosophy " affords not better : for under the person of Bacchus is described the nature of affection, passion, or perturbation, the mother of which (though never so hurtful) is nothing else but the object of apparent good in the eyes of appetite. And it is always conceived in an unlawful desire rashly propounded and obtained, before well understood and considered, and when it begins to grow, the mother of it, which is the desire of apparent good, by too much fervency is destroyed and perisheth : nevertheless, whilst it is yet an imperfect embryo, it is nourished and preserved in the human soul (which is, as it were, a father unto it, and represented by Jupiter), but especially in the inferior parts thereof, as in a thigh, where also it causeth so much trouble and vexation as that good determinations and actions are much hindered and lamed thereby, and when it comes to be confirmed by consent and habit, and breaks out, as it were, into act, it remains yet a while with Proserpina, as with a nurse ; that is, it seeks corners and secret places, and, as it were, caves under ground, until (the reigns of shame and fear being laid aside in a pampered audaciousness) it either takes the pretext of some virtue or becomes altogether impudent and shameless. And it is most true, that every vehement passion is of a doubtful sex, as being masculine in the first motion, but feminine in the prosecution.

It is an excellent fiction that of Bacchus' reviving; for passions do sometimes seem to be in a dead sleep, and, as it were, utterly extinct, but we should not think them to be so, indeed; no, though they lay, as it were, in their grave; for let there be but matter and opportunity offered, and you shall see them quickly to revive again.

The invention of wine is wittily ascribed unto him, every affection being ingenious and skilful in finding out that which brings nourishment unto it; and, indeed, of all things known to men, wine is most powerful and efficacious to excite and kindle passions of what kind soever, as being in a manner a common nurse to them all.

Again, his conquering of nations and undertaking infinite expeditions is an excellent device; for desire never rests content with what it hath, but with an infinite and insatiable appetite still covets and gapes after more.

His chariot also is well said to be drawn by tigers; for as soon as any affection shall, from going a foot, be advanced to ride in a chariot, and shall captivate reason and lead her in a triumph, it grows cruel, untamed, and fierce against whatsoever withstands or opposeth it.

It is worth the noting also, that those ridiculous hobgoblins are brought in, dancing about his chariot; for every passion doth cause, in the eyes, face, and gesture, certain indecent and ill-seeming, apish, and deformed motions, so that they who in any kind of passion, as in anger, arrogancy, or love, seem glorious and brave in their own eyes, do yet appear to others misshapen and ridiculous.

In that the Muses are said to be of his company, it shows that there is no affection almost which is not soothed by some art, wherein the indulgence of wits doth derogate from the glory of the Muses, who (when they ought to be the mistresses of life) are made the waiting maids of affections.

Again, where Bacchus is said to have loved Ariadne that was rejected by Theseus, it is an allegory of special observation; for it is most certain that passions always covet and desire that which experience forsakes, and they all know (who have paid dear for serving and obeying their lusts) that whether it be honour, or riches, or delight, or glory, or knowledge, or anything else which they seek after, yet are they but things cast off, and by divers men in all ages, after experience had, utterly rejected and loathed.

Neither is it without a mystery that the ivy was sacred to Bacchus, for the application holds; first, in that the ivy remains green in winter; secondly, in that it sticks to, embraceth, and overtoppeth so many divers bodies, as trees, walls, and edifices. Touching the first, every passion doth by resistance and reluctation, and, as it were, by an Antiparistasis (like the ivy of the cold of winter) grow fresh and lusty. And as for the other, every predominate affection doth again (like the ivy) embrace and limit all human actions and determinations, adhering and cleaving fast unto them.

Neither is it a wonder that superstitious rites and ceremonies were attributed unto Bacchus, seeing every giddy-headed humour keeps, in a manner, revel rout in false religions; or that the cause of madness should be ascribed unto him, seeing every affection is by nature a short fury, which, if it grow vehement and become habitual, concludes madness.

Concerning the rending and dismembering of Pentheus and Orpheus the parable is plain, for every prevalent affection is outrageous and severe against curious inquiry and wholesome and free admonition.

Lastly, that confusion of Jupiter and Bacchus, their persons, may be well transferred to a parable, seeing noble and famous acts, and remarkable and glorious merits, do sometimes proceed from virtue and well-ordered reason and magnanimity, and sometimes from a secret affection and hidden passion, which are so dignified with the celebrity of fame and glory that a man can hardly distinguish between the acts of Bacchus and the jests of Jupiter.

XXV.

ATALANTA, OR GAIN.

ATALANTA, who was reputed to excel in swiftness, would needs challenge Hippomanes at a match in running. The conditions of the prize were these: That if Hippomanes won the race, he should espouse Atalanta; if he were outrun, that then he should forfeit his life. And in the opinion of all, the victory was thought assured of Atalanta's side, being famous as she was for her matchless and inconquerable speed, whereby she had been the bane of many. Hippomanes therefore bethinks him how to deceive her by a trick, and in that regard provides three golden apples, or balls, which he purposely carried about him. The race is begun, and Atalanta gets a good start before him. He seeing himself thus cast behind, being mindful of his device, throws one of his golden balls before her, and yet not outright, but somewhat on the one side, both to make her linger, and also to draw her out of the right course; she, out of a womanish desire (being thus enticed with the beauty of the golden apple), leaving her direct race, runs aside, and stoops to catch the ball; Hippomanes the while holds on his course, getting thereby a great start, and leaves her behind him; but she, by her own natural swiftness, recovers her lost time, and gets before him again. But Hippomanes still continues his sleight, and both the second and third times casts out his balls, those enticing delays; and so by craft and not by his activity wins the race and victory.

This fable seems allegorically to demonstrate a notable conflict between art and nature; for art, signified by Atalanta, in its work—if it be not let and hindered—is far more swift than nature, more speedy in pace, and sooner attains the end it aims at, which is manifest almost in every effect; as you may see in fruit-trees, whereof those that grow of a kernel are long ere they bear, but such as are grafted on a stock a great deal sooner. You may see it in clay, which, in the generation of stones, is long ere it become hard, but in the burning of bricks is very quickly effected. Also in moral passages you may observe that it is a long time ere, by the benefit of nature, sorrow can be assuaged and comfort attained, whereas philosophy—which is, as it were, the art of living—tarries not the leisure of time, but doth it instantly and out of hand. And yet this prerogative and singular agility of art is hindered by certain golden apples, to the infinite prejudice of human proceedings; for there is not any one art or science which constantly perseveres in a true and lawful course till it come to the proposed end or mark: but ever and anon makes stops after good beginnings, leaves the race, and turns aside to profit and commodity, like Atalanta.

"*Declinat cursus, aurumque volubile tollit.*"

"Who doth her course forsake,
The rolling gold to take."

And therefore it is no wonder that art hath not the power to conquer nature, and by pact or law of conquest to kill and destroy her; but, on the contrary, it falls out that art becomes subject to nature, and yields the obedience, as of a wife to her husband.

XXVI.

PROMETHEUS, OR THE STATE OF MAN.

THE ancients deliver that Prometheus made a man of clay, mixed with certain parcels taken from divers animals, who, studying to maintain this his work by art—that he might not be accounted a founder only, but a propagator of human kind—stole up to heaven with a bundle of twigs, which he kindled at the chariot of the sun, came down again, and communicated it with men; and yet they say that, notwithstanding this excellent work of his, he was requited with ingratitude in a treacherous conspiracy: for they accused both him and his invention to Jupiter, which was not so taken as was meet it should, for the information was pleasing to Jupiter and all the gods; and therefore in a merry mood granted unto men, not only the use of fire, but perpetual youth also—a boon most acceptable and desirable. They being, as it were,

D—15

overjoyed, did foolishly lay this gift of the gods upon
the back of an ass, who, being wonderfully oppressed
with thirst, and near a fountain, was told by a serpent,
which had the custody thereof, that he should not
drink unless he would promise to give him the burden
that was on his back. The silly ass accepted the condition, and so the restoration of youth, sold for a
draught of water, passed from men to serpents. But
Prometheus, full of malice, being reconciled unto men
after they were frustrated of their gift, but in a chafe
yet with Jupiter, feared not to use deceit in sacrifice;
for having killed two bulls, and in one of their hides
wrapped up the flesh and fat of them both, and in the
other only the bones, with a great show of religious
devotion, gave Jupiter his choice, who, detecting his
fraud and hypocrisy, but taking an occasion of revenge,
chose that that was stuffed with bones, and so turning
to revenge (when he saw that the insolence of Prometheus would not be repressed but by laying some
grievous affliction upon mankind, in the forming of
which he so much bragged and boasted), commanded
Vulcan to frame a goodly beautiful woman, which
being done, every one of the gods bestowed a gift
on her, whereupon she was called Pandora. To this
woman they gave in her hand a goodly box, full of all
miseries and calamities, only in the bottom of it they
put hope. With this box she comes first to Prometheus,
thinking to catch him if, peradventure, he should
accept it at her hands, and so open it; which he,
nevertheless, with good providence and foresight

refused. Whereupon she goes to Epimetheus, who, though brother to Prometheus, yet was of a much differing disposition, and offers this box unto him, who, without delay, took it and rashly opened it, but when he saw that all kinds of miseries came fluttering about his ears, being wise too late, with great speed and earnest endeavour clapped on the cover, and so, with much ado, retained hope sitting alone in the bottom. At last Jupiter, laying many and grievous crimes to Prometheus his charge—as, namely, that he had stolen fire from heaven, that in contempt of his majesty he sacrificed a bull's hide stuffed with bones, that he scornfully rejected his gift, and besides all this that he offered violence to Pallas—cast him into chains, and doomed him to perpetual torment; and by Jupiter's command he was brought to the mountain Caucasus, and there bound fast to a pillar, that he could not stir; there came an eagle also, that every day sat tearing upon his liver, and wasted it, but as much as was eaten in the day grew again in the night, that matter for torment to work upon might never decay. But yet they say there was an end of this punishment; for Hercules crossing the ocean in a cup which the sun gave him, came to Caucasus, and set Prometheus at liberty by shooting the eagle with an arrow. Moreover, in some nations there were instituted, in the honour of Prometheus, certain games of lamp-bearers, in which they that strived for the prize were wont to carry lighted torches, which whoso suffered to go out yielded the place and victory to those that followed, and so cast back themselves, so that whosoever came first to the mark with his torch burning got the prize.

This fable demonstrates and presseth many true and grave speculations, wherein some things have been heretofore well noted, others not so much as touched.

Prometheus doth clearly and eminently signify Providence; for in the universality of nature the fabric and constitution of man only was by the ancients picked out and chosen and attributed unto Providence as a peculiar work. The reason of it seems to be not only in that the nature of man is capable of a mind and understanding which is the seat of Providence, and therefore it would seem strange and incredible that the reason and mind should so proceed and flow from dumb and deaf principles, as that it should necessarily be concluded the soul of man to be endued with providence, not without the example, intention, and stamp of a greater providence. But this also is chiefly propounded that man is, as it were, the centre of the world, in respect of final causes, so that if man were not in nature, all things would seem to stray and wander without purpose, and like scattered branches, as they say, without inclination to their end. For all things attend on man, and he makes use of and gathers fruit from all creatures; for the revolutions and periods of stars make both for the distinctions of times and the distribution of the world's site. Meteors also are referred to as the presages of tempests; and winds are ordained as well for navigation as for turning of mills and other engines; and plants, and animals of what kind soever, are useful either for men's houses and places of shelter, or for raiment, or food, or medicine, or for ease of labour, or, in a word, for delight and solace, so that all things seem to work, not for themselves, but for man.

Neither is it added without consideration that certain particles were taken from divers living creatures, and mixed and tempered with that classic mass, because it is most true that of all things comprehended within the compass of the universe, man is a thing most mixed and compounded, insomuch that he was well termed by the ancients "A Little World;" for although the Chymics do, with too much curiosity, take and wrest the elegancy of this word—Microcosm—to the letter, contending to find in man all minerals, all vegetables, and the rest, or anything that holds proportion with them, yet this proposition remains sound and whole, that the body of man, of all material beings, is found to be most compounded, and most organical, whereby it is endued and furnished with most admirable virtues and faculties. And as for simple bodies, their powers are not many, though certain and violent, as existing without being weakened, diminished, or stinted by mixture; for the multiplicity and excellency of operation have their residence in mixture and composition, and yet, nevertheless, man in his originals seems to be a thing unarmed, and naked, and unable to help itself, as needing the aid of many things; therefore Prometheus made haste to find out fire, which suppeditates and yields comfort and help in a manner to all human wants and necessities; so that if the soul be the form of forms, if the hand be the instrument of instruments, fire deserves well to be called the succour of succours, or the help of helps, which infinite ways affords aid and assistance to all labours and mechanical arts, and to the sciences themselves.

The manner of stealing this fire is aptly described, even from the nature of the thing. It was, as they say, by a bundle of twigs held to touch the chariot of the sun; for twigs are used in giving blows or stripes, to signify clearly that fire is engendered by the violent percussion and mutual collision of bodies, by which their material substances are attenuated and set in motion, and prepared to receive the heat or influence of the heavenly bodies, and so, in a clandestine manner, and, as it were, by stealth, may be said to take and snatch the fire from the chariot of the sun.

There follows next a remarkable part of the parable: that men, instead of gratulation and thanksgiving, were angry, and expostulated the matter with Prometheus, insomuch that they accused both him and his invention unto Jupiter, which was so acceptable unto him that he augmented their former commodities with a new bounty. Seems it not strange that ingratitude towards the author of a benefit (a vice that in a manner contains all other vices) should find such approbation and reward? No, it seems to be otherwise; for the meaning of the allegory is this: That men's outcries upon the defects of nature and art proceed from an excellent disposition of the mind, and turn to their good; whereas, the silencing of them is hateful to the gods, and redounds not so much to their profit. For they that infinitely extol human nature, or the knowledge they possess, breaking out into a prodigal admiration of that they have and enjoy, adoring also those sciences they profess, would have them be accounted perfect. They do, first of all, show little reverence to the divine nature, by equalising, in a manner, their own defects with God's perfection. Again, they are wonderfully injurious to men, by imagining they have attained the highest step of knowledge, and so resting themselves contented, seek no farther. On the contrary, such as bring nature and art to the bar with accusations and bills of complaint against them, are indeed of more true and moderate judgments; for they are ever in action, seeking always to find out new inventions, which makes me much to wonder at the foolish and inconsiderate dispositions of some men, who, making themselves bond-slaves to the arrogancy of a few, have the philosophy of the Peripatetics (containing only a portion of Grecian wisdom, and that but a small one neither) in so great esteem, that they hold it, not only an unprofitable but a suspicious and almost heinous thing, to lay any imputation of imperfection upon it. I approve rather of Empedocles in his opinion, who, like a madman, and of Democritus in his judgment, who with great moderation, complained how that all things were involved in a mist that we knew nothing, that we discerned nothing, that truth was drowned in the depths of obscurity, and that false things were wonderfully joined and intermixed with true (as for the new Academy that exceeded all measure), than of the confident and pronunciative school of Aristotle. Let men therefore be admonished, that by acknowledging the imperfections of nature and art, they are grateful to the gods, and shall thereby obtain new benefits and greater favours at their bountiful hands; and the accusation of Prometheus, their author and master, though bitter and vehement, will conduce more to their profit, than to be effuse in the congratulation of his invention; for, in a word, the opinion of having enough is to be accounted one of the greatest causes of having too little.

Now, as touching the kind of gift which men are said to have received in reward of their accusation (to wit, an everlasting flower of youth), it is to show that the ancients seemed not to despair of attaining the skill, by means and medicines, to put off old age, and to prolong life; but this to be numbered rather among such things as (having been once happily attained unto) are now through men's negligence and carelessness, utterly perished and lost, than among such as have been always denied and never granted. For they signify and show that, by affording the true use of fire, and by a good and stern accusation and conviction of the errors of art, the divine bounty is not wanting unto men in the obtaining of such gifts, but men are wanting to themselves in laying this gift of the gods upon the back of a silly and slow-paced ass, which may seem to be experience, a stupid thing, and full of delay, from whose leisurely and snail-like pace proceeds that complaint of life's brevity and art's length. And to say the truth, I am of this opinion : that those two faculties, dogmatical and empirical, are not as yet well joined and coupled together, but as new gifts of the gods imposed either upon philosophical abstractions, as upon a flying bird, or upon slow and dull experience, as upon an ass. And yet, methinks, I would not entertain an ill conceit of this ass, if it flinch not for the accidents of travail and thirst; for I am persuaded that, whoso constantly goes on by the conduct of experience, as by a certain rule and method, and not covets to meet with such experiments by the way, as conduce either to gain or ostentation (to obtain which he must be fain to lay down and sell this burden), may prove no unfit porter to bear this new addition of divine munificence.

Now, in that this gift is said to pass from men to serpents, it may seem to be added to the fable for ornament's sake in a manner, unless it were inserted to shame men that, having the use of that celestial fire, and of many arts, are not able to get unto themselves such things as nature itself bestows upon many other creatures.

But that sudden reconciliation of men to Prometheus, after they were frustrated of their hopes, contains a profitable and wise note, showing the levity and temerity of men in new experiments; for if they have not present success answerable to their expectation, they will with too sudden haste desist from that they began, and with precipitancy returning to their former experiments, are reconciled to them again.

The state of man in respect of arts, and such things as concern the intellect, being now described, the parable passeth to religion. For after the planting of arts follows the setting of divine principles, which hypocrisy hath overspread and polluted. By that two-fold sacrifice, therefore, is elegantly shadowed out the persons of a true religious man and an hypocrite. In the one is contained fatness, which, by reason of the inflammation and fumes thereof, is called the portion of God, by which his affection and zeal, tending to God's glory, and ascending towards heaven, is signified. In Him also are contained the bowels of charity, and in Him is found that good and wholesome flesh. Whereas, in the other, there is nothing but dry and naked bones, which nevertheless do stuff up the hide, and make it appear like a fair and goodly sacrifice. By this may well be meant those external and vain rites and empty ceremonies by which men do oppress and fill up the sincere worship of God, things composed rather for ostentation, than any way conducing to true piety. Neither do they hold it sufficient to offer such mock sacrifices unto God, except they also lay them before Him, as if He had chosen and bespoke them. Certainly, the prophet in the person of God, doth thus expostulate concerning his choice (Isaiah lviii. 5). "*Num tandem hoc est illud jejunium quod elegi, ut homo animam suam in diem unum affligat, et caput instar junci demittat?*" "Is it such a fast that I have chosen, that a man should afflict his soul for a day, and to bow down his head like a bulrush ?,"

Having now touched the state of religion, the parable converts itself to the manners and conditions of human life. And it is a common but apt interpretation, by Pandora to be meant pleasure and voluptuousness, which (when the civil life is pampered with too much art and culture and superfluity) is engendered, as it were, by the efficacy of fire, and therefore the work of voluptuousness is attributed unto Vulcan, who also himself doth represent fire. From this do infinite miseries, together with too late repentance proceed, and overflow the minds, bodies, and fortunes of men, and that not only in respect of particular estates, but even over kingdoms and commonwealths; for from this fountain have wars, and tumults, and tyrannies derived their origin.

But it would be worth the labour to consider how elegantly and proportionably this fable doth delineate two conditions, or, as I may say, two tables or examples of human life, under the persons of Prometheus and Epimetheus; for they that are of Epimetheus's sect are improvident, not foreseeing what may come to pass hereafter, esteeming that best which seems most sweet for the present; whence it happens that they are overtaken with many miseries, difficulties, and calamities, and so lead their lives almost in perpetual affliction; but yet, notwithstanding they please their fancy, and out of ignorance of the passages of things, do entertain many vain hopes in their mind, whereby they sometimes, as with sweet dreams, solace themselves, and sweeten the miseries of their life. But they that are Prometheus's scholars are men endued with prudence, warily foreseeing things to come, shunning and avoiding many evils and misfortunes. But to these their good properties they have this also annexed, that they deprive themselves and defraud their genius of many lawful pleasures and divers recreations, and, which is worse, they vex and torment themselves with cares and troubles, and intestine fears. For, being chained to the pillar of necessity, they are afflicted with innumerable cogitations (which, because they are very swift, may be fitly compared to an eagle), and those griping, and, as it were, gnawing and devouring the liver, unless sometimes, as it were by night, it may be they get a little recreation and ease of mind, but so as that they are again suddenly assaulted with fresh anxieties and fears.

Therefore, this benefit happens to but a very few of either condition, that they should retain the commodities of providence, and free themselves from the miseries of care and perturbation; neither, indeed, can any attain unto it but by the assistance of Hercules, that is, fortitude and constancy of mind, which is prepared for every event, and armed in all fortunes, foreseeing without fear, enjoying without loathing, and suffering without impatience. It is worth the noting also, that this virtue was not natural to Prometheus, but adventitious, and from the indulgence of another; for no inbred and natural fortitude is able to encounter with these miseries. Moreover, this virtue was received and brought unto him from the remotest part of the ocean, and from the sun, that is, from wisdom, as from the sun, and from the meditation of inconstancy, or of the waters of human life, as from the sailing upon the ocean, which, too, Virgil hath well enjoined in these verses :—

> " *Felix qui potuit rerum cognoscere causas ;*
> *Quique metus omnes, et inexorabile fatum,*
> *Subjecit pedibus, strepitumque Acherontis avari.*"

> " Happy is he that knows the cause of things,
> And that with dauntless courage treads upon
> All fear and fates, relentless threatenings,
> And greedy throat of roaring Acheron."

Moreover, it is elegantly added for the consolation and confirmation of men's minds, that this noble hero crossed the ocean in a cup or pan, lest peradventure, they might too much fear that the straits and frailty of their nature will not be capable of this fortitude and constancy. Of which very thing Seneca well conceived when he said, " *Magnum est habere simul fragilitatem hominis et securitatem Dei.*" It is a great matter for human frailty and divine security to be one and the selfsame time in one and the selfsame subject.

But now we are to step back a little to that, which by premeditation we passed over, lest a breach should be made in those things that were so linked together.

That, therefore, which I would touch here, is that last crime imputed to Prometheus, about seeking to bereave Minerva of her virginity; for questionless, it was this heinous offence that brought that punishment of devouring his liver upon him, which is nothing else but to show that when we are puffed up with much learning and science, they go about oftentimes to make even divine oracles subject to sense and reason, whence most certainly follows a continual distraction and restless griping of the mind; we must, therefore, with a sober and humble judgment, distinguish between humanity and divinity, and between the oracles of sense and the mysteries of faith, unless an heretical religion and a commentitious philosophy be pleasing unto us.

Lastly, it remains that we say something of the games of Prometheus performed with burning torches, which again hath reference to arts and sciences, as that fire, in whose memory and celebration these games were instituted; and it contains in it a most wise admonition, that the perfection of sciences is to be expected from succession, not from the nimbleness and promptness of one only author; for they that are nimblest in course, and strongest in contention, yet happily have not the luck to keep fire still in their torch; seeing it may be as well extinguished in running too fast as by going too slow. And this running and contending with lamps seems long since to be intermitted, seeing all sciences seem even now to flourish most in their first authors, Aristotle, Galen, Euclid, and Ptolemy, succession having neither effected, nor almost attempted any great matter. It were therefore to be wished that these games in honour of Prometheus or human nature were again restored, and that matters should receive success by combat and emulation, and not hang upon any one man's sparkling and shaking torch. Men therefore are to be admonished to rouse up their spirits and try their strength and turns, and not refer all to the opinions and brains of a few.

And thus have I delivered that which I thought good to observe out of this so well-known and common fable; and yet I will not deny but that there may be some things in it which have an admirable consent with the mysteries of Christian religion, and especially that sailing of Hercules in a cup, to set Prometheus at liberty, seems to represent an image of the Divine Word coming in flesh as in a frail vessel to redeem man from the slavery of hell. But I have interdicted my pen all liberty in this kind, lest I should use strange fire at the altar of the Lord.

XXVII.

SCYLLA AND ICARUS, OR THE MIDDLE-WAY.

MEDIOCRITY or the middle-way is most commended in moral actions, in contemplative sciences not so celebrated, though no less profitable and commodious; but in political employments to be used with great heed and judgment. The ancients by the way prescribed to Icarus, noted the mediocrity of manners; and by the way between Scylla and Charybdis, so famous for difficulty and danger, the mediocrity of intellectual operations.

Icarus being to cross the sea by flight, was commanded by his father that he should fly neither too high nor too low; for his wings being joined with wax, if he should mount too high, it was to be feared, lest the wax would melt by the heat of the sun; and if too low, lest the misty vapours of the sea would make it less tenacious. But he, in a youthful jollity soaring too high, fell down headlong and perished in the water.

The parable is easy and vulgar; for the way of virtue lies in a direct path between excess and defect. Neither is it a wonder that Icarus perished by excess, seeing that excess, for the most part, is the peculiar fault of youth, as defect is of age, and yet of two evil and hurtful ways, youth commonly makes choice of the better, defect being always accounted worst; for whereas excess contains some sparks of magnanimity, and like a bird claims kindred of the heavens, defect, only like a base worm, crawls upon the earth. Excellently, therefore, said Heraclitus, "*Lumen siccum optima anima*"—"A dry light is the best soul;" for if the soul contract moisture from the earth, it becomes degenerate altogether. Again, on the other side, there must be moderation used, that this light be subtilised by this laudable fixity, and not destroyed by too much fervency. And thus much every man, for the most part, knows.

Now, they that would sail between Scylla and Charybdis must be furnished as well with the skill as prosperous success of navigation; for if their ships fall into Scylla, they are split on the rocks; if into Charybdis, they are swallowed up of a gulf.

The moral of this parable, which we will but briefly touch, although it contains matter of infinite contemplation, seems to be this, that in every art and science, and so in their rules and axioms, there be a mean observed between the rocks of distinctions and the gulfs of universalities, which two are famous for the wrecks both of wits and arts.

XXVIII.

SPHYNX, OR SCIENCE.

THEY say that Sphynx was a monster of divers forms, as having the face and voice of a virgin, the wings of a bird, and the talons of a griffon. Her abode was in a mountain, near the city of Thebes. She kept also the highways, and used to lie in ambush for travellers, and so to surprise them; to whom, being in her power, she propounded certain dark and intricate riddles, which were thought to have been given and received of the Muses. Now, if these miserable captives were not able instantly to resolve and interpret them, in the midst of their difficulties and doubts, she would rend and tear them in pieces. The country groaning a long time under this calamity, the Thebans at last propounded the kingdom as a reward unto him that could interpret the riddles of Sphynx, there being no other way to destroy her. Whereupon Œdipus (a man of piercing and deep judgment, but maimed and lame by reason of holes bored in his feet), moved with the hope of so great a reward, accepted the condition, and determined to put it to the hazard; and so, with an undaunted and bold spirit, presented himself before the monster, who, asking him what creature that was which, after his birth, went first upon four feet, next upon two, then upon three, and lastly upon four again, answered forthwith that it was

Man, which, in his infancy, immediately after birth, crawls upon all four, scarce venturing to creep; and not long after, stands upright upon two feet; then growing old, he leans upon a staff wherewith he supports himself, so that he may seem to have three feet; and at last, in decrepit years, his strength failing him, he falls grovelling again upon four, and lies bed-ridden. Having, therefore, by this true answer, gotten the victory, he slew this Sphynx, and (laying her body upon an ass) led it, as it were, in triumph: and so (according to the condition) was created king of the Thebans.

This fable contains in it no less wisdom than elegancy, and it seems to point at science, especially that which is joined with practice; for science may not absurdly be termed a monster, as being by the ignorant and rude multitude always held in admiration.

It is divers in shape and figure by reason of the infinite variety of subjects wherein it is conversant. A maiden face and voice is attributed unto it for its gracious countenance and volubility of tongue. Wings are added because sciences and their inventions do pass and fly from one or another, as it were, in a moment, seeing that the communication of science is as the kindling of one light at another. Elegantly also is it feigned to have sharp talons, because the axioms and arguments of science do so fasten upon the mind, and so strongly apprehend and hold it, as that it cannot stir or evade, which is noted also by the divine philosopher (Eccl. xii. 11). "*Verba sapientum*" (saith he),

"*sunt tanquam aculei et veluti clavi in altum defixi*"—
"The words of the wise are like goads, and like nails
driven far in."

Moreover, all science seems to be placed in steep and
high mountains, as being thought to be a lofty and high
thing, looking down upon ignorance with a scornful
eye. It may be observed and seen also a great way
and far in compass, as things set on the tops of
mountains.

Farthermore, science may well be feigned to beset
the highways, because which way so ever we turn in
this progress and pilgrimage of human life, we meet
with some matter or occasion offered for contemplation.

Sphynx is said to have received from the Muses
divers difficult questions and riddles, and to propound
them unto men, which, remaining with the Muses, are
free (it may be) from savage cruelty: for, so long as
there is no other end of study and meditation than to
know, the understanding is not racked and imprisoned,
but enjoys freedom and liberty, and even in doubts and
variety finds a kind of pleasure and delectation; but
when once enigmas are delivered by the Muses to the
Sphynx, that is, to practice, so that it be solicited and
urged by action, and election, and determination, then
they begin to be troublesome and raging; and unless
they be resolved and expedited, they do wonderfully
torment and vex the minds of men, distracting, and in
a manner rending them into sundry parts.

Moreover, there is always a two-fold condition

propounded with Sphynx's enigmas : to him that doth not expound them, distraction of mind ; and to him that doth, a kingdom : for he that knows that which he sought to know, hath attained the end he aimed at, and every artificer also commands over his work.

Of Sphynx her riddles, there are generally two kinds : some concerning the nature of things, others touching the nature of man. So also there are two kinds of emperies, as rewards to those that resolve them : the one over nature, the other over men ; for the proper and chief end of true natural philosophy is to command and sway over natural beings, as bodies, medicines, mechanical works and infinite other things ; although the school (being content with such things as are offered, and priding itself with speeches) doth neglect realities, and works, treading them, as it were, under foot. But that enigma propounded to Œdipus (by means of which he obtained the Theban empire) belonged to nature of man ; for whosoever doth thoroughly consider the nature of man, may be in a manner the contriver of his own fortune, and is born to command, which is well spoken of the Roman arts.

"*Tu regere imperio populos, Romane memento,*
   Hæ tibi erunt artes."

"Roman, remember that with sceptre's awe
   Thy realms thou rule. These arts let be thy law."

It was therefore very apposite that Augustus Cæsar

(whether by premeditation or by chance) bare a Sphynx in his signet, for he (if ever any) was famous not only in political government, but in all the course of his life. He happily discovered many new enigmas concerning the nature of man, which if he had not done with dexterity and promptness, he had oftentimes fallen into imminent danger and destruction.

Moreover, it is added in the fable that the body of Sphynx when she was overcome was laid upon an ass, which indeed is an elegant fiction, seeing there is nothing so acute and abstruse but (being well understood and divulged) may be apprehended by a slow capacity.

Neither is it to be omitted that Sphynx was overcome by a man lame in his feet; for when men are too swift of foot, and too speedy of pace in having to Sphynx her enigmas, it comes to pass that (she getting the upper hand) their wits and minds are rather distracted by disputations than that ever they come to command by works and effects.

XXIX.

PROSERPINA, OR SPIRIT.

PLUTO, they say, being made king of the infernal dominions (by that memorable division), was in despair of
ever attaining any one of the superior goddesses in
marriage, especially if he should venture to court them
either with words or with any amorous behaviour, so that
of necessity he was to lay some plot to get one of them
by rapine; taking therefore the benefit of opportunity
he caught up Proserpina the daughter of Ceres, a beautiful virgin, as she was gathering narcissus flowers in
the meadows of Sicily, and carried her away with him
in his coach to the subterranean dominions, where she
was welcomed with such respect, as that she was styled
the Lady of Dis. But Ceres her mother, when in no
place she could find this her only beloved daughter, in
a sorrowful humour and distracted beyond measure,
went compassing the whole earth with a burning torch
in her hand to seek and recover this her lost child. But
when she saw that all was in vain, supposing peradventure that she was carried to hell, she importuned Jupiter
with many tears and lamentations, that she might be
restored unto her again, and at length prevailed thus
far, that if she had tasted of nothing in hell, she should
have leave to bring her from thence, which condition
was as good as a denial to her petition, Proserpina
having already eaten three grains of a pomegranate.

And yet for all this, Ceres gave not over her suit, but fell to prayers and moans afresh. Wherefore it was at last granted (the year being divided) Proserpina should by alternate courses remain one six months with her husband, and other six months with her mother. Not long after this, Theseus and Perithous in an over-hardy adventure attempted to fetch her from Pluto's bed, who being weary with travel and sitting down upon a stone in hell to rest themselves, had not the power to rise again, but sate there for ever. Proserpina therefore remained queen of hell, in whose honour there was this great privilege granted, that although it were enacted that none who went down to hell should have the power ever to return from thence, yet was this singular exception annexed to this law, that if any presented Proserpina with a golden bough, it should be lawful for him to come and go at his pleasure. Now there was but one only such bough in a spacious and shady grove, which was not a plant neither of itself, but budded from a tree of another kind like a rope of gum, which being plucked off, another would instantly spring out.

This fable seems to pertain to nature, and to dive into that rich and plentiful efficacy and variety of subalternal creatures, from whom whatsoever we have is derived, and to them doth again return.

By Proserpina the ancients meant that ethereal spirit which (being separated from the upper globe) is shut up and detained under the earth (represented by Pluto), which the poet well expressed thus.

> "*Sive recens Tellus seductaque nuper ab alto*
> *Æthere, cognati retinebat semina cœli.*"

> "Whether the youngling Tellus, that of late
> Was from the high-reared Æther separate,
> Did yet contain her teeming womb within
> The living seeds of Heaven, her nearest kin."

This spirit is feigned to be rapted by the earth, because nothing can withhold it when it hath time and leisure to escape. It is therefore caught and stayed by a sudden contraction, no otherwise than if a man should go about to mix air with water, which can be done by no means but by a speedy and rapid agitation, as may be seen in froth, wherein the air is rapted by the water.

Neither is it inelegantly added that Proserpina was rapted as she was gathering narcissus flowers in the valleys, because Narcissus hath his name from slowness, or stupidity; for, indeed, then is this spirit most prepared and fitted to be snatched by terrestrial matter, when it begins to be coagulated, and becomes, as it were, slow.

Rightly is Proserpina honoured more than any of the other gods' bed-fellows in being styled the Lady of Dis, because this spirit doth rule and sway all things in those lower regions, Pluto abiding stupid and ignorant.

This spirit, the power celestial (shadowed by Ceres) strives with infinite sedulity to recover and get again; for that brand, or burning torch of Æther (which Ceres carried in her hand), doth doubtless signify the sun, which enlighteneth the whole circuit of the earth, and would be of greatest moment to recover Proserpina, if possibly it might be.

But Proserpina abides still, the reason of which is accurately and excellently propounded in the conditions between Jupiter and Ceres; for, first, it is most certain there are two ways to keep spirit in solid and terrestrial matter—the one by constipation or obstruction, which is mere imprisonment and constraint; the other by administration of proportionable nutriment, which it receives willingly and of its own accord; for after that the included spirit begins to feed and nourish itself, it makes no haste to be gone, but is, as it were, linked to its earth. And this is pointed at by Proserpina, her eating of a pomegranate, which if she had not done, she had long since been recovered by Ceres with her torch, compassing the earth. Now, as concerning that spirit which is in metals and minerals, it is chiefly, perchance, restrained by the solidity of mass; but that which is in plants and animals inhabits a porous body, and hath open passage to be gone in a manner as it lists, were it not that it willingly abides of its own accord, by reason of the relish it finds in its entertainment. The second condition concerning the six months' custom, it is no other than an elegant description of the division of the year, seeing this spirit mixed with the earth appears above ground in vegetable bodies during the summer months, and in the winter sinks down again.

Now, as concerning Theseus and Perithous, their attempt to bring Proserpina quite away, the meaning of it is, that it oftentimes comes to pass that some more subtle spirits, descending with divers bodies to the earth, never come to suck of any subalternal spirit, whereby to unite it unto them, and so to bring it away; but, on the contrary, are coagulated themselves, and never rise more, that Proserpina should be by that means augmented with inhabitants and dominion.

All that we can say concerning that spring of gold is hardly able to defend us from the violence of the Chymics, if in this regard they set upon us, seeing they promise by that their elixir to effect golden mountains and the restoring of natural bodies, as it were, from the portal of hell. But concerning chemistry, and those perpetual suitors for that philosophical elixir, we know, certainly, that their theory is without grounds, and we suspect that their practice also is without certain reward. And therefore, omitting these, of this last part of the parable this is my opinion. I am induced to believe by many figures of the ancients that the conservation and restoration of natural bodies in some sort was not esteemed by them as a thing impossible to be attained, but as a thing abstruse and full of difficulties; and so they seem to intimate in this place, when they report that this one only sprig was found among infinite other trees in a huge and thick wood, which they feigned to be of gold, because gold is the badge of perpetuity, and to be artificially, as it were, inserted, because this effect is to be rather hoped for from art than from any medicine, or simple or natural means.

XXX.

METIS, OR COUNSEL.

THE ancient poets report that Jupiter took Metis to wife, whose name doth plainly signify counsel, and that she by him conceived, which, when he found, not tarrying the time of her deliverance, he devoured both her and that which she went withal, by which means Jupiter himself became with child, and was delivered of a wondrous birth, for out of his head or brain came forth Pallas armed.

The sense of this fable (which at first apprehension may seem monstrous and absurd) contains in it a secret of state, to wit, with what policy kings are wont to carry themselves towards their counsellors, whereby they may not only preserve their authority and majesty free and entire, but also that it may be the more extolled and dignified of the people. For kings being, as it were, tied and coupled in a nuptial bond to their counsellors, do truly conceive that communicating with them about the affairs of greatest importance they do yet detract nothing from their own majesty. But when any matter comes to be censured or decreed (which is as a birth), there do they confine and restrain the liberty of their counsellors, lest that which is done should seem to be hatched by their wisdom and judgment. So as at last kings, except it be in such matters as are distasteful and maligned, which they always will be sure to put off from themselves, do assume the honour and praise of all matters that are ruminated in counsel, and, as it were, formed in the womb, whereby the resolution and execution (which, because it proceeds from power, and implies a necessity, is elegantly shadowed under the figure of Pallas armed) shall seem to proceed wholly from themselves. Neither sufficeth it that it is done by the authority of the king, by his mere will and free applause, except withal this be added and appropriated as to issue out of his own head or brain, intimating that out of his own judgment, wisdom, and ordinance it was only invented and derived.

XXXI.

THE SIRENS, OR PLEASURES.

THE fable of the Sirens seems rightly to have been applied to the pernicious allurements of pleasure, but in a very vulgar and gross manner. And therefore to

me it appears that the wisdom of the ancients has
with a farther reach or insight strained deeper matter
out of them; not unlike to grapes ill-pressed, from
which, though some liquor were drawn, yet the best
was left behind. These Sirens are said to be the
daughters of Achelous and Terpsichores, one of the
Muses, who, in their first being, were winged, but
after rashly entering into contention with the Muses,
were by them vanquished and deprived of their wings,
of whose plucked-out feathers the Muses made themselves coronets; so as ever since that time all the Muses
have attired themselves with plumed heads, except
Terpsichores only, that was mother to the Sirens.
The habitation of the Sirens was in certain pleasant
islands, from whence, as soon as out of their watch-
tower they discovered any ships approaching, with
their sweet tunes they would first entice and stay them,
and having them in their power, would destroy them.
Neither was their song plain and single, but consisting
of such variety of melodious tunes, so fitting and
delighting the ears that heard them, as that it ravished
and betrayed all passengers. And so great was the
mischief they did, that these isles of the Sirens, even
as far off as a man could ken them, appeared all over
white with the bones of unburied carcases. For the
remedying of this misery, a double means was at last
found out—the one by Ulysses, the other by Orpheus.
Ulysses (to make experiment of his device) caused all
the ears of his company to be stopped with wax, and
made himself to be bound to the mainmast, with

special commandment to his mariners not to be loosed, albeit himself should require them so to do; but Orpheus, neglecting and disdaining to be so bound, with a shrill and sweet voice singing the praises of the gods to his harp, suppressed the songs of the Sirens, and so freed himself from their danger.

This fable hath relation to men's manners, and contains in it a manifest and most excellent parable; for pleasures do for the most part proceed out of the abundance and superfluity of all things, and also out of the delights and jovial contentments of the mind, the which are wont suddenly, as it were, with winged enticements to ravish and rapt mortal men. But learning and education brings it so to pass, as that it strains and bridles man's mind, making it so to consider the ends and events of things, as that it clips the wings of pleasure. And this was greatly to the honour and renown of the Muses; for after that by some examples it was made manifest that by the power of philosophy vain pleasures might grow contemptible, it presently grew to great esteem as a thing that could raise and elevate the mind aloft that seemed to be base and fixed to the earth, and make the cogitations of men (which do ever reside in the head), to be ethereal, and, as it were, winged. But that the mother of the Sirens was left to her feet and without wings, that, no doubt, is no otherwise meant than of light and superficial learning, appropriated and defined only to pleasures as were those which Petronius devoted himself unto, after he had received his fatal sentence, and having his foot, as it were, upon the threshold of death, sought to give himself all delightful contentments, insomuch as when he had caused consolatory letters to be sent him, he would peruse none of them (as Tacitus reports) that should give him courage and constancy, but only read fantastical verses, such as these are :—

> *" Vivamus, mea Lesbia atque amemus,*
> *Rumoresque senium severiorum*
> *Omnes unius æstimemus assis. "*

> " My Lesbia, let us live and love ;
> Though wayward dotards us reprove,
> Weigh their words light for our behove."

And this also :—

> *" Iura senes norint, et quid sit fasque nefasque*
> *Inquirant tristes, legumque examina servent."*

> " Let doting grandsires know the law,
> And right and wrong observe with awe,
> Let them in that strict circle draw."

This kind of doctrine would easily persuade to take these plumed coronets from the Muses, and so restore the wings again to the Sirens. These Sirens are said to dwell in remote isles, for that pleasures love privacy and retired places, shunning always too much company of people. The Siren songs are so vulgarly understood, together with the deceits and danger of them, as that they need no exposition. But that of the bones appearing like white cliffs and described afar off hath more acuteness in it. For thereby is signified, that albeit the examples of afflictions be manifest and eminent, yet do they not sufficiently deter us from the wicked enticements of pleasures.

As for the remainder of this parable, though it be not over mystical, yet is it very grave and excellent, for in it are set out three remedies for this violent enticing mischief; to wit, two from philosophy, and one from religion. The first means to shun these inordinate pleasures is, withstand and resist them in their beginnings, and seriously to shun all occasions that are offered to debauch and entice the mind, which is signified in that stopping of the ears, and that remedy is properly used by the meaner and baser sort of people, as it were Ulysses' followers or mariners. Whereas more heroic and noble spirits may boldly converse even in the midst of these seducing pleasures, if with a resolved constancy they stand upon their guard, and fortify their minds; and so take greater contentment in the trial and experience of this their approved virtue, learning rather thoroughly to understand the follies and vanities of those pleasures by contemplation, than by submission. Which Solomon avouched of himself when he reckoning up the multitude of those solaces and pleasures wherein he swam, doth conclude with this sentence:

"*Sapientia quoque perseveravit mecum.*"
"Wisdom also continued with me."

Therefore these heroes and spirit of this excellent temper, even in the midst of these enticing pleasures,

E—15

can show themselves constant and invincible, and are able to support their own virtuous inclination, against all heady and forcible persuasions whatsoever, as by the example of Ulysses that so peremptorily interdicted all pestilent counsels and flatteries of his companions as the most dangerous and pernicious poisons to captivate the mind. But of all other remedies in this case, that of Orpheus is most predominant; for that they chant and resound the praises of the gods, confound and dissipate the voices and incantations of the Sirens, for divine meditations do not only in power subdue all sensual pleasures, but also far exceed them in sweetness and delight.

NEW ATLANTIS.

NEW ATLANTIS.

———◆———

WE sailed from Peru (where we had continued by the space of one whole year), for China and Japan, by the South Sea, taking with us victuals for twelve months; and had good winds from the east, though soft and weak, for five months' space and more; but then the wind came about, and settled in the west for many days, so as we could make little or no way, and were sometimes in purpose to turn back. But then again there arose strong and great winds from the south, with a point east, which carried us up, for all that we could do, towards the north, by which time our victuals failed us, though we had made good spare of them. So that finding ourselves in the midst of the greatest wilderness of waters in the world, without victual, we gave ourselves for lost men, and prepared for death. Yet we did lift up our hearts and voices to God above, who showeth His wonders in the deep, beseeching Him of His mercy, that as in the beginning He discovered the face of the deep, and brought forth dry land, so

He would now discover land to us, that we might
not perish. And it came to pass that the next day,
about evening, we saw within a kenning* before us, towards the north, as it were, thick clouds, which did put
us in some hope of land, knowing how that part of the
South Sea was utterly unknown, and might have
islands, or continents, that hitherto were not come to
light.† Wherefore we bent our course thither, where

* *A kenning*, as far as one can see. John Palsgrave, in
" Lesclarcissement de la Langue Francoyse " (1530), explains
"Je blanchis " by " I am within syght, as a shyppe is that
cometh within the kennyng."

† *Islands, or continents, that hitherto were not come to light.*
Existing maps, of which the earliest is in the British Museum,
prove that the Portuguese had as early as 1540 a belief that
there was much land in the region now known as Australia.
It is figured south of Java as a great region called, " Jave la
Grande." A map by a Jean Rotz, in an English volume of
1542, repeats this representation, calling the great southern
continent " The Londe of Java," and Java " The Lytil Java."
In the Introduction to Mr. R. H. Major's edition for the
Hakluyt Society (1859) of " Early Voyages to Terra Australis,
now called Australia," will be found very interesting results of
an inquiry into the growth from suspicion to vague knowledge
of the existence of an unexplored Austral land, of which it was
said in a book by Cornelius Wytfliet, published at Louvain, in
1598, that "its shores are hitherto but little known, since
after one voyage and another, that route has been deserted,
and seldom is the country visited unless when sailors are
driven there by storms. The Australis Terra begins at two or
three degrees from the equator, and is maintained by some to
be of so great an extent that if it were thoroughly explored,

we saw the appearance of land all that night; and in the dawning of the next day we might plainly discern that it was a land, flat to our sight, and full of boscage;* which made it show the more dark. And after an hour and a half sailing, we entered into a good haven, being the port of a fair city—not great, indeed. but well built, and that gave a pleasant view from the sea. And we, thinking every minute long till we were on land, came close to the shore, and offered to land; but straightways we saw divers of the people, with bastons in their hands, as it were, forbidding us to land; yet without any cries of fierceness, but only as warning us off by signs that they made. Whereupon. being not a little discomfited, we were advising with ourselves what we should do; during which time there made forth to us a small boat with about eight persons in it, whereof one of them had in his hand a tipstaff of a yellow cane, tipped at both ends with blue, who came aboard our ship without any show of distrust at all.

it would be regarded as a fifth part of the world." In 1606 a part of the Australian coast was visited by the Dutch yacht, the *Duyphen*. In the same year, Luis Vaez de Torres, a Spaniard, passed through Torres Straits, which separate Australia from New Guinea. Bacon's knowledge went no farther, but the Dutch were busy in the southern seas during the last years of his life, and in 1642, fourteen years after his death, began the discoveries of Abel Jans Tasman.

* *Boscage*, wood, thicket. An old French word; modern French, "bocage." So, a little later, *bastons*, sticks or staves, *bâtons*.

And when he saw one of our number present himself somewhat afore the rest, he drew forth a little scroll of parchment (somewhat yellower than our parchment, and shining like the leaves of writing-tables, but otherwise soft and flexible), and delivered it to our foremost man. In which scroll were written in ancient Hebrew, and in ancient Greek, and in good Latin of the school, and in Spanish, these words: "Land ye not, none of you; and provide to be gone from this coast within sixteen days, except you have further time given you. Meanwhile, if you want fresh water, or victual, or help for your sick, or that your ship needeth repair, write down your wants, and you shall have that which belongeth to mercy." This scroll was signed with a stamp of cherubims' wings, not spread, but hanging downwards; and by them a cross. This being delivered, the officer returned, and left only a servant with us to receive our answer. Consulting hereupon amongst ourselves, we were much perplexed. The denial of landing and hasty warning us away troubled us much; on the other side to find that the people had languages, and were so full of humanity, did comfort us not a little. And above all, the sign of the cross to that instrument was to us a great rejoicing, and, as it were, a certain presage of good. Our answer was in the Spanish tongue: "That for our ship, it was well, for we had rather met with calms and contrary winds than any tempests; for our sick, they were many, and in very ill case, so that if they were not permitted to land they ran danger of their lives." Our other wants we set down in particular; adding, that we had some little store of merchandise, which, if it pleased them to deal for, it might supply our wants without being chargeable unto them. We offered some reward in pistolets * unto the servant, and a piece of crimson velvet to be presented to the officer; but the servant took them not, nor would scarce look upon them; and so left us, and went back in another little boat, which was sent for him.

About three hours after we had despatched our answer, there came towards us a person (as it seemed) of place. He had on him a gown with wide sleeves, of a kind of water chamolett,† of an excellent azure colour, far more glossy than ours. His under apparel was green, and so was his hat, being in the form of a turban, daintily made, and not so huge as the Turkish turbans, and the locks of his hair came down below the brims of it—a reverend man was he to behold. He came in a boat, gilt in some part of it, with four persons more only in that boat; and was followed by another boat, wherein were some twenty. When he

---

* *Pistolets* were gold coins two grains lighter than ducats. The ducat weighed 2 dwt. 6 gr. There were also double pistolets and double ducats.

† *Chamolett*, chamlet or camlet. Spanish " camelote " and " chamelote," a stuff originally made of camels' hair, afterwards of hair and silk, and then of wool and thread. It had a wavy or watered gloss, and in the latest cheapened form was used as a material for cloaks comparatively waterproof, until the application of caoutchouc to other fabrics.

was come within a flight-shot of our ship, signs were
made to us that we should send forth some to meet
him upon the water, which we presently * did in our
ship-boat, sending the principal man amongst us save
one, and four of our number with him. When we
were come within six yards of their boat, they called to
us to stay, and not to approach farther, which we did.
And thereupon the man whom I before described stood
up, and with a loud voice, in Spanish, asked, "Are ye
Christians?" We answered we were; fearing the
less because of the cross we had seen in the subscrip-
tion. At which answer the said person lifted up his
right hand towards Heaven, and drew it softly to his
mouth (which is the gesture they use when they thank
God), and then said, "If ye will swear, all of you, by
the merits of the Saviour, that ye are no pirates, nor
have shed blood, lawfully nor unlawfully, within forty
days past, you may have license to come on land."
We said we were all ready to take that oath. Whereupon, one of those that were with him, being, as it
seemed, a notary, made an entry of this act. Which
done, another of the attendants of the great person,
which was with him in the same boat, after his lord
had spoken a little to him, said aloud, "My lord would
have you know that it is not of pride or greatness that
he cometh not aboard your ship, but for that, in your
answer, you declare that you have many sick amongst
you, he was warned by the Conservator of Health of

---

* *Presently*, immediately.

the city that he should keep a distance." We bowed ourselves towards him and answered, "We were his humble servants, and accounted for great honour and singular humanity towards us that which was already done; but hoped well that the nature of the sickness of our men was not infectious." So he returned; and awhile after came the notary to us aboard our ship, holding in his hand a fruit of that country, like an orange, but of colour between orange-tawny and scarlet, which cast a most excellent odour; he used it, as it seemeth, for a preservative against infection. He gave us our oath, by the name of Jesus and His merits, and after told us that the next day, by six of the clock in the morning, we should be sent to, and brought to the Strangers' House (so he called it), where we should be accommodated of things, both for our whole and for our sick. So he left us; and when we offered him some pistolets, he smiling said, "He must not be twice paid for one labour;" meaning, as I take it, that he had salary sufficient of the State for his service. For, as I after learned, they call an officer that taketh rewards, twice paid.

The next morning early there came to us the same officer that came to us at first with his cane, and told us he came to conduct us to the Strangers' House, and that he had prevented* the hour because we might

* *Prevented*, come before, the strict meaning of the word. As in the prayer to God in one of the Collects of the English Church that His grace "may always prevent and follow us."

have the whole day before us for our business. "For," said he, "if you will follow my advice, there shall first go with me some few of you, and see the place, and how it may be made convenient for you; and then you may send for your sick, and the rest of your number, which ye will bring on land." We thanked him, and said, "That this care which he took of desolate strangers God would reward." And so six of us went on land with him. And when we were on land he went before us, and turned to us and said, "He was but our servant and our guide." He led us through three fair streets, and all the way we went there were gathered some people on both sides, standing in a row, but in so civil a fashion, as if it had been not to wonder at us, but to welcome us. And divers of them, as we passed by them, put their arms a little abroad, which is their gesture when they bid any welcome. The Strangers' House is a fair and spacious house, built of brick, of somewhat a bluer colour than our brick, and with handsome windows, some of glass, some of a kind of cambric oiled. He brought us first into a fair parlour above stairs, and then asked us what number of persons we were, and how many sick? We answered, "We were in all (sick and whole) one and fifty persons, whereof our sick were seventeen." He desired us to have patience a little, and to stay till he came back to us, which was about an hour after; and then he led us to see the chambers which were provided for us, being in number nineteen. They having cast it (as it seemeth) that four of those chambers, which were better than

the rest, might receive four of the principal men of
our company, and lodge them alone by themselves; and
the other fifteen chambers were to lodge us two and
two together. The chambers were handsome and
cheerful chambers, and furnished civilly. Then he led
us to a long gallery, like a dorture,* where he showed
us all along the one side (for the other side was but
wall and window) seventeen cells, very neat ones,
having partitions of cedar wood, which gallery and
cells, being in all forty (many more than we needed),
were instituted as an infirmary for sick persons. And
he told us withal, that as any of our sick waxed well,
he might be removed from his cell to a chamber, for
which purpose there were set forth ten spare chambers
besides the number we spake of before. This done, he
brought us back to the parlour, and lifting up his cane
a little (as they do when they give any charge or command), said to us, " Ye are to know that the custom of
the land requireth that after this day and to-morrow
(which we give you for removing of your people from
your ship) you are to keep within doors for three days.
But let it not trouble you, nor do not think yourselves
restrained, but rather left to your rest and ease. You
shall want nothing, and there are six of our people appointed to attend you for any business you may have
abroad." We gave him thanks with all affection and
respect, and said, "God surely is manifested in this

---

* *Dorture*, from French "dortoir," Latin "dormitorium,"
dormitory.

land." We offered him also twenty pistolets; but he
smiled, and only said, "What? twice paid!" and so
he left us. Soon after our dinner was served in, which
was right good viands, both for bread and meat, better
than any collegiate diet that I have known in Europe.
We had also drink of three sorts, all wholesome and
good: wine of the grape, a drink of grain (such as is
with us our ale, but more clear), and a kind of cider
made of a fruit of that country—a wonderful pleasing
and refreshing drink. Besides, there were brought in
to us great store of those scarlet oranges for our sick,
which, they said, were an assured remedy for sickness
taken at sea. There was given us also a box of small
grey, or whitish, pills, which they wished our sick
should take, one of the pills every night before sleep,
which, they said, would hasten their recovery. The
next day, after that our trouble of carriage, and removing of our men and goods out of our ship was
somewhat settled and quiet, I thought good to call our
company together, and when they were assembled, said
unto them, "My dear friends,—Let us know ourselves,
and how it standeth with us. We are men cast on
land, as Jonas was, out of the whale's belly, when we
were as buried in the deep; and now we are on land.
We are but between death and life, for we are beyond
both the old world and the new; and whether ever we
shall see Europe, God only knoweth. It is a kind of
miracle hath brought us hither, and it must be little
less that shall bring us hence. Therefore, in regard of
our deliverance past, and our danger present and to

come, let us look up to God, and every man reform his
own ways.   Besides, we are come here amongst a
Christian people, full of piety and humanity; let us
not bring that confusion of face upon ourselves, as to
show our vices or unworthiness before them.   Yet
there is more, for they have by commandment (though
in form of courtesy) cloistered us within these walls for
three days; who knoweth whether it be not to take
some taste of our manners and conditions?   And if
they find them bad, to banish us straightways; if good,
to give us further time; for these men that they have
given us for attendance may withal have an eye upon
us.   Therefore, for God's love, and as we love the weal
of our souls and bodies, let us so behave ourselves as
we may be at peace with God, and may find grace in
the eyes of this people."   Our company with one voice
thanked me for my good admonition, and promised me
to live soberly and civilly, and without giving any the
least occasion of offence.   So we spent our three days
joyfully and without care, in expectation what would
be done with us when they were expired; during
which time we had every hour joy of the amendment
of our sick, who thought themselves cast into some
divine pool of healing, they mended so kindly and so
fast.

The morrow after our three days were passed there
came to us a new man, that we had not seen before,
clothed in blue, as the former was, save that his turban
was white, with a small red cross on the top; he had
also a tippet of fine linen.   At his coming in he did

bend to us a little, and put his arms abroad. We on our parts saluted him in a very lowly and submissive manner, as looking that from him we should receive sentence of life or death. He desired to speak with some few of us, whereupon six of us only stayed, and the rest avoided the room. He said: "I am by office governor of this House of Strangers, and by vocation I am a Christian priest, and, therefore, am come to you to offer you my service, both as strangers and chiefly as Christians. Some things I may tell you, which, I think, you will not be unwilling to hear. The State hath given you license to stay on land for the space of six weeks; and let it not trouble you if your occasions ask further time, for the law in this point is not precise; and I do not doubt but myself shall be able to obtain for you such further time as may be convenient. Ye shall also understand that the Strangers' House is at this time rich, and much aforehand, for it hath laid up revenue these thirty-seven years, for so long it is since any stranger arrived in this part. And, therefore, take ye no care; the State will defray you all the time you stay; neither shall you stay one day the less for that. As for any merchandise ye have brought, ye shall be well used, and have your return either in merchandise or in gold and silver, for to us it is all one. And if you have any other request to make, hide it not, for ye shall find we will not make your countenance to fall by the answer ye shall receive. Only this I must tell you, that none of you must go above a karan [that is with them a mile and a half]

from the walls of the city without especial leave."
We answered, after we had looked awhile one upon
another, admiring this gracious and parent-like usage,
that we could not tell what to say, for we wanted words
to express our thanks, and his noble, free offers left us
nothing to ask. It seemed to us that we had before us
a picture of our salvation in Heaven : for we that were
a while since in the jaws of death were now brought
into a place where we found nothing but consolations.
For the commandment laid upon us we would not fail
to obey it, though it was impossible but our hearts
should be inflamed to tread further upon this happy
and holy ground. We added, "That our tongues should
first cleave to the roofs of our mouths ere we should
forget either his reverend person or this whole nation
in our prayers." We also most humbly besought him
to accept of us as his true servants, by as just a right
as ever men on earth were bounden, laying and pre-
senting both our persons and all we had at his feet.
He said he was a priest, and looked for a priest's reward, which was our brotherly love and the good of
our souls and bodies. So he went from us—not without tears of tenderness in his eyes—and left us also
confused with joy and kindness, saying amongst ourselves, that we were come into a land of angels, which
did appear to us daily, and prevent us with comforts
which we thought not of, much less expected.

The next day, about ten of the clock, the governor
came to us again, and, after salutations, said familiarly,
that he was come to visit us; and called for a chair,

and sat him down. And we, being some ten of us (the
rest were of the meaner sort, or else gone abroad), sat
down with him. And when we were sat, he began
thus: "We, of this island of Bensalem [for so they
call it in their language], have this: That by means of
our solitary situation, and the laws of secrecy which
we have for our travellers, and our rare admission of
strangers, we know well most part of the habitable
world, and are ourselves unknown. Therefore, because
he that knoweth least is fittest to ask questions, it is
more reason for the entertainment of the time that ye
ask me questions than that I ask you." We answered,
that we humbly thanked him that he would give us
leave so to do, and that we conceived by the taste we
had already that there was no worldly thing on earth
more worthy to be known than the state of that happy
land. But above all, we said, since that we were met
from the several ends of the world, and hoped assuredly
that we should meet one day in the kingdom of Heaven
(for that we were both parts Christians), we desired to
know (in respect that that land was so remote, and so
divided by vast and unknown seas from the land where
our Saviour walked on earth) who was the Apostle of
that nation, and how it was converted to the faith?
It appeared in his face that he took great contentment in this our question. He said: "Ye knit my
heart to you by asking this question in the first place,
for it showeth that you first seek the kingdom of
Heaven, and I shall gladly and briefly satisfy your
demand.

"About twenty years after the Ascension of our Saviour, it came to pass that there was seen by the people of Renfusa (a city upon the eastern coast of our island) within night (the night was cloudy and calm), as it might be some mile into the sea, a great pillar of light, not sharp, but in form of a column or cylinder, rising from the sea a great way up towards Heaven; and on the top of it was seen a large cross of light, more bright and resplendent than the body of the pillar. Upon which so strange a spectacle, the people of the city gathered apace together upon the sands to wonder, and so after put themselves into a number of small boats, to go nearer to this marvellous sight. But when the boats were come within (about) sixty yards of the pillar they found themselves all bound, and could go no further; yet so as they might move to go about, but might not approach nearer. So as the boats stood all as in a theatre, beholding this light as a heavenly sign, it so fell out that there was in one of the boats one of the wise men of the Society of Salomon's House, which house, or college, my good brethren, is the very eye of this kingdom, who, having awhile attentively and devoutly viewed and contemplated this pillar and cross, fell down upon his face, and then raised himself upon his knees, and lifting up his hands to Heaven, made his prayers in this manner :—

"'Lord God of Heaven and earth, Thou hast vouchsafed of Thy grace to those of our order to know Thy works of creation and the secrets of them, and to discern (as far as appertaineth to the generations of men) between divine miracles, works of nature, works of art, and impostures and illusions of all sorts. I do here acknowledge and testify before this people that the thing which we now see before our eyes is Thy finger, and a true miracle. And forasmuch as we learn in our books that Thou never workest miracles but to a divine and excellent end (for the laws of nature are Thine own laws, and Thou exceedest them not but upon great cause), we most humbly beseech Thee to prosper this great sign, and to give us the interpretation and use of it in mercy, which Thou dost in some part secretly promise by sending it unto us.'

" When he had made his prayer, he presently found the boat he was in movable and unbound, whereas all the rest remained still fast; and taking that for an assurance of leave to approach, he caused the boat to be softly, and with silence, rowed towards the pillar; but ere he came near it the pillar and cross of light brake up, and cast itself abroad, as it were, into a firmament of many stars, which also vanished soon after, and there was nothing left to be seen but a small ark, or chest of cedar, dry, and not wet at all with water, though it swam. And in the fore end of it, which was towards him, grew a small green branch of palm; and when the wise man had taken it, with all reverence, into his boat, it opened of itself, and there were found in it a book and a letter, both written on fine parchment, and wrapped in sindons * of linen. The book contained all the canonical books of the Old and New Testament, according as you have them (for we know well what the churches with you receive), and the Apocalypse itself, and some other books of the New Testament, which were not at that time written, were nevertheless in the book. And for the letter, it was in these words :—

" ' I, Bartholomew, † a servant of the Highest, and Apostle of Jesus Christ, was warned by an angel, that appeared to me in a vision of glory, that I should commit this ark to the floods of the sea. Therefore, I do testify and declare unto that people where God shall ordain this ark to come to land, that in the same day has come unto them salvation and peace, and goodwill from the Father and from the Lord Jesus.'

" There was also in both these writings, as well the book as the letter, wrought a great miracle, like to that of the Apostles in the original gift of tongues.

---

* *Sindons.* Sindon is a classical word (Greek, "σινδὼν") for a fine Indian cotton stuff. As a delicate and soft fabric, it was fit for enveloping delicate and costly things (as we now might use cotton-wool). Sindons meant, therefore, delicate wrappings ; and the word is still used in surgery for the plug of soft cotton put, to protect the brain, into the hole made in the skull by use of the trephine.

† *Bartholomew* is the saint named, because church legend associated him with the work of spreading the tidings of the Gospel to far lands. He was said to have preached in Greater Armenia, to have converted the Lycaonians, and to have at last carried the Gospel into India, whence he never returned.

For there being at that time in this land Hebrews,
Persians, and Indians, besides the natives, every one
read upon the book and letter, as if they had been
written in his own language. And thus was this land
saved from infidelity (as the remains of the Old World
were from water) by an ark, through the Apostolical
and miraculous evangelism of Saint Bartholomew."
And here he paused, and a messenger came and called
him from us. So this was all that passed in that
conference.

The next day the same governor came again to us
immediately after dinner, and excused himself, saying
that the day before he was called from us somewhat
abruptly, but now he would make us amends, and
spend time with us if we held his company and conference agreeable. We answered, "That we held it so
agreeable and pleasing to us as we forgot both dangers
past and fears to come for the time we heard him
speak. And that we thought an hour spent with him
was worth years of our former life." He bowed himself
a little to us, and after we were set again, he said,
"Well, the questions are on your part." One of our
number said, after a little pause, that there was a
matter we were no less desirous to know than fearful
to ask, lest we might presume too far; but, encouraged
by his rare humanity towards us (that could scarce
think ourselves strangers, being his vowed and pro-
fessed servants), we would take the hardiness to propound it, humbly beseeching him, if he thought it not
fit to be answered, that he would pardon it though he

rejected it. We said, we well observed those his
words which he formerly spake, that this happy island
where we now stood was known to few, and yet knew
most of the nations of the world; which we found to
be true, considering they had the languages of Europe,
and knew much of our state and business, and yet we
in Europe (notwithstanding all the remote discoveries
and navigations of this last age) never heard any of
the least inkling or glimpse of this island. This we
found wonderful strange, for that all nations have
inter-knowledge one of another, either by voyage into
foreign parts, or by strangers that come to them. And
though the traveller into a foreign country doth
commonly know more by the eye than he that stayeth
at home can by relation of the traveller, yet both ways
suffice to make a mutual knowledge in some degree on
both parts. But for this island, we never heard tell of
any ship of theirs that had been seen to arrive upon
any shore of Europe; no, nor of either the East or
West Indies, nor yet of any ship of any other part of
the world that had made return from them. And yet
the marvel rested not in this, for the situation of it (as
his lordship said) in the secret conclave * of such a
vast sea might cause it. But then, that they should
have knowledge of the languages, books, affairs of
those that lie such a distance from them, it was a

* *Conclave*, a room or space that may be locked up. From
Latin "con," with, and "clavis," a key. Hence the present
use of the word for a secret council.

thing we could not tell what to make of; for that it seemed to us a condition and propriety of divine powers and beings to be hidden and unseen to others, and yet to have others open and as in a light to them. At this speech the governor gave a gracious smile, and said, "That we did well to ask pardon for this question we now asked, for that it imported as if we thought this land a land of magicians, that sent forth spirits of the air into all parts to bring them news and intelligence of other countries." It was answered by us all in all possible humbleness, but yet with a countenance taking knowledge that we knew that he spake it but merrily. That we were apt enough to think there was something supernatural in this island, but yet rather as angelical than magical. But to let his lordship know truly what it was that made us tender, and doubtful to ask this question, it was not any such conceit, but because we remembered he had given a touch in his former speech that this land had laws of secrecy touching strangers. To this he said: "You remember it aright, and therefore in that I shall say to you I must reserve some particulars which it is not lawful for me to reveal; but there will be enough left to give you satisfaction.

"You shall understand—that which, perhaps, you will scarce think credible—that about three thousand years ago, or somewhat more, the navigation of the world (especially for remote voyages) was greater than at this day. Do not think with yourselves that I know not how much it is increased with you within these

six score years; I know it well, and yet I say greater
then than now. Whether it was that the example of
the ark that saved the remnant of men from the
universal deluge gave men confidence to adventure
upon the waters, or what it was, but such is the
truth. The Phœnicians, and specially the Tyrians,
had great fleets; so had the Carthaginians their
colony, which is yet further west. Towards the East
the shipping of Egypt and of Palestina was likewise
great; China, also, and the great Atlantis (that
you call America), which have now but junks and
canoes, abounded then in tall ships. This island (as
appeareth by faithful registers of those times) had
then fifteen hundred strong ships of great content. Of
all this there is with you sparing memory, or none;
but we have large knowledge thereof.

"At that time this land was known and frequented
by the ships and vessels of all the nations before
named. And, as it cometh to pass, they had many
times men of other countries, that were no sailors, that
came with them: as Persians, Chaldeans, Arabians.
So as almost all nations of might and fame resorted
hither, of whom we have some stirps* and little tribes
with us at this day. And for our own ships, they went
sundry voyages, as well to your Straits, which you call
the Pillars of Hercules,† as to other parts in the

* *Stirps*, progeny. Latin, "stirps," stem, plant, shoot, stock,
race, offspring : used here as in Virgil's "stirps et genus omne
futurum."

† Straits of Gibraltar.

Atlantic and Mediterranean Seas; as to Paguin (which is the same with Cambaline) * and Quinzy, † upon the Oriental seas, as far as to the borders of the East Tartary.

"At the same time, and an age after or more, the inhabitants of the Great Atlantis did flourish. For though the narration and description which is made by a great man with you, that the descendants of Neptune planted there, and of the magnificent temple, palace, city, and hill, and the manifold streams of goodly navigable rivers (which as so many chains environed the same site and temple), and the several degrees of ascent, whereby men did climb up to the same, as if it had been a Scala Cœli, ‡ be all poetical and fabulous, yet so much is true that the said country of Atlantis—as well that of Peru, then called Coya, as that of Mexico, then named Tyrambel—were mighty and proud kingdoms in arms, shipping, and riches; so mighty as at one time—or at least within the space of ten years—they both made two great expeditions: they of Tyrambel through the Atlantic to the Mediterranean Sea; and they of Coya through the South Sea upon this our island. And for the former of these, which was into Europe, the same author amongst you, as it seemeth, had some relation

---

* Cambay, in Gujerat, where trade has decayed by shallowing of the Gulf of Cambay.

† *Quinzy*, the Chinese province of Quang-si.

‡ Stair of Heaven.

from the Egyptian priest whom he citeth, for assuredly such a thing there was. But whether it were the ancient Athenians that had the glory of the repulse and resistance of those forces, I can say nothing; but certain it is, there never came back either ship or man from that voyage. Neither had the other voyage of those of Coya upon us had better fortune, if they had not met with enemies of greater clemency. For the king of this island, by name Altabin, a wise man and a great warrior, knowing well both his own strength and that of his enemies, handled the matter so as he cut off their land forces from their ships, and entoiled both their navy and their camp with a greater power than theirs, both by sea and land, and compelled them to render themselves without striking stroke. And after they were at his mercy, contenting himself only with their oath that they should no more bear arms against him, dismissed them all in safety. But the divine revenge overtook not long after those proud enterprises, for within less than the space of one hundred years the great Atlantis was utterly lost and destroyed, Not by a great earthquake, as your man saith (for that whole tract is little subject to earthquakes), but by a particular deluge, or inundation, those countries having at this day far greater rivers and far higher mountains to pour down waters than any part of the Old World. But it is true that the same inundation was not deep: not past forty feet in most places from the ground; so that although it destroyed man and beast generally, yet some few wild inhabitants of the wood escaped, birds also were saved by flying to the high trees and woods. For, as for men, although they had buildings in many places higher than the depth of the water, yet that inundation, though it were shallow, had a long continuance, whereby they of the vale that were not drowned perished for want of food and other things necessary. So as marvel you not at the thin population of America, nor at the rudeness and ignorance of the people, for you must account your inhabitants of America as a young people, younger a thousand years at the least than the rest of the world; for that there was so much time between the universal flood and their particular inundation. For the poor remnant of human seed which remained in their mountains peopled the country again slowly by little and little : and being simple and savage people (not like Noah and his sons, which was the chief family of the earth), they were not able to leave letters, arts, and civility to their posterity. And having likewise in their mountainous habitations been used (in respect of the extreme cold of those regions) to clothe themselves with the skins of tigers, bears, and great hairy goats that they have in those parts, when after they came down into the valley, and found the intolerable heats which are there, and knew no means of lighter apparel, they were forced to begin the custom of going naked, which continueth at this day. Only they take great pride and delight in the feathers of birds; and this also they took from those their ancestors of the mountains, who were invited unto it by the infinite flights of birds that came up to the high grounds while the waters stood below. So you see, by this main accident of time, we lost our traffic with the Americans, with whom, of all others, in regard they lay nearest to us, we had most commerce. As for the other parts of the world, it is most manifest that in the ages following (whether it were in respect of wars, or by a natural revolution of time) navigation did everywhere greatly decay, and especially far voyages (the rather by the use of galleys, and such vessels, as could hardly brook the ocean) were altogether left and omitted. So then, that part of intercourse which could be from other nations to sail to us, you see how it hath long since ceased, except it were by some rare accident as this of yours. But now of the cessation of that other part of intercourse which might be by our sailing to other nations, I must yield you some other cause; for I cannot say, if I shall say truly, that our shipping for number, strength, mariners, pilots, and all things that appertain to navigation, is as great as ever; and, therefore, why we should sit at home, I shall now give you an account by itself; and it will draw nearer to give you satisfaction to your principal question.

"There reigned in this island about 1,900 years ago a king, whose memory of all others we most adore: not superstitiously, but as a divine instrument though a mortal man. His name was Solamona, and we esteem him as the law-giver of our nation. This king had a large heart, inscrutable for good, and was

wholly bent to make his kingdom and people happy.
He, therefore, taking into consideration how sufficient
and substantive this land was to maintain itself without any aid at all of the foreigner; being 5,600 miles
in circuit, and of rare fertility of soil in the greatest
part thereof: and finding also the shipping of this
country might be plentifully set on work, both by
fishing and by transportations from port to port, and
likewise by sailing unto some small islands that are
not far from us, and are under the crown and laws of
this State: and recalling into his memory the happy
and flourishing estate wherein this land then was, so as
it might be a thousand ways altered to the worse, but
scarce any one way to the better—thought nothing
wanted to his noble and heroical intentions, but only
(as far as human foresight might reach) to give
perpetuity to that which was in his time so happily
established.   Therefore, amongst his other fundamental
laws of this kingdom, he did ordain the interdicts and
prohibitions which we have touching entrance of
strangers, which, at that time (though it was after the
calamity of America) was frequent, doubting novelties
and commixture of manners.   It is true, the like law
against the admission of strangers without license is
an ancient law in the kingdom of China, and yet continued in use; but there it is a poor thing, and hath
made them a curious, ignorant, fearful, foolish nation.
But our law-giver made his law of another temper.
For first, he hath preserved all points of humanity in
taking order and making provision for the relief of

strangers distressed, whereof you have tasted." At which speech, as reason was, we all rose up and bowed ourselves. He went on: "That king also, still desiring to join humanity and policy together, and thinking it against humanity to detain strangers here against their wills, and against policy that they should return and discover their knowledge of this estate, he took this course: he did ordain that of the strangers that should be permitted to land, as many at all times might depart as would; but as many as would stay should have very good conditions and means to live from the State. Wherein he saw so far, that now, in so many ages since the prohibition, we have memory not of one ship that ever returned, and but of thirteen persons only, at several times, that chose to return in our bottoms. What those few that returned may have reported abroad I know not; but you must think whatsoever they have said could be taken, where they came, but for a dream. Now for our travelling from hence into parts abroad, our law-giver thought fit altogether to restrain it. So is it not in China, for the Chinese sail where they will or can, which showeth that their law of keeping out strangers is a law of pusillanimity and fear. But this restraint of ours hath one only exception, which is admirable: preserving the good which cometh by communicating with strangers, and avoiding the hurt. And I will now open it to you; and here I shall seem a little to digress, but you will by-and-bye find it pertinent.

"Ye shall understand, my dear friends, that

amongst the excellent acts of that king, one above all
hath the pre-eminence. It was the erection and
institution of an order, or society, which we call
Salomon's House: the noblest foundation, as we
think, that ever was upon the earth, and the lanthorn
of this kingdom. It is dedicated to the study of the
works and creatures of God. Some think it beareth
the founder's name a little corrupted, as if it should be
Solamona's House, but the records write it as it is
spoken. So as I take it to be denominate of the king
of the Hebrews, which is famous with you and no
stranger to us, for we have some parts of his works
which with you are lost; namely, that Natural History
which he wrote of all Plants, from the cedar of Libanus
to the moss that groweth out of the wall, and of all
things that have life and motion. This maketh me
think that our king, finding himself to symbolise in
many things with that king of the Hebrews (which
lived many years before him), honoured him with the
title of this foundation. And I am the rather induced
to be of this opinion for that I find in ancient records
this order, or society, is sometimes called Salomon's
House, and sometimes the College of the Six Days'
Works, whereby I am satisfied that our excellent king
had learned from the Hebrews that God had created
the world and all that therein is within six days; and
therefore, he instituting that house for the finding out
of the true nature of all things (whereby God might
have the more glory in the workmanship of them, and
men the more fruit in the use of them), did give it also

that second name. But now to come to our present
purpose. When the king had forbidden to all his
people navigation into any part that was not under his
crown, he made, nevertheless, this ordinance: that
every twelve years there should be set forth out of this
kingdom two ships appointed to several voyages; that
in either of these ships there should be a mission of
three of the fellows, or brethren, of Salomon's House,
whose errand was only to give us knowledge of the
affairs and state of those countries to which they were
designed, and especially of the sciences, arts, manu-
factures, and inventions of all the world; and withal
to bring unto us books, instruments, and patterns in
every kind. That the ships, after they had landed the
brethren, should return, and that the brethren should
stay abroad till the new mission. These ships are not
otherwise fraught than with store of victuals, and good
quantity of treasure to remain with the brethren, for
the buying of such things and rewarding of such
persons as they should think fit. Now for me to tell
you how the vulgar sort of mariners are contained from
being discovered at land, and how they that must be
put on shore for any time colour themselves under
the names of other nations, and to what places these
voyages have been designed, and what places of
rendezvous are appointed for the new missions, and the
like circumstances of the practice—I may not do it.
Neither is it much to your desire. But thus you see
we maintain a trade, not for gold, silver, or jewels;
not for silks, not for spices, nor any other commodity

F—15

of matter; but only for God's first creature, which was Light. To have light, I say, of the growth of all parts of the world."

And when he had said this he was silent, and so were we all; for indeed we were all astonished to hear so strange things so probably told. And he, perceiving that we were willing to say somewhat but had it not ready, in great courtesy took us off, and descended to ask us questions of our voyage and fortunes, and in the end concluded that we might do well to think with ourselves what time of stay we would demand of the State; and bade us not to scant ourselves, for he would procure such time as we desired. Whereupon we all rose up, and presented ourselves to kiss the skirt of his tippet, but he would not suffer us, and so took his leave. But when it came once amongst our people that the State used to offer conditions to strangers that would stay, we had work enough to get any of our men to look to our ship, and to keep them from going presently to the governor to crave conditions. But with much ado we refrained them till we might agree what course to take.

We took ourselves now for free men, seeing there was no danger of our utter perdition, and lived most joyfully, going abroad, and seeing what was to be seen in the city, and places adjacent within our tether; and obtaining acquaintance with many of the city, not of the meanest quality, at whose hands we found such humanity, and such a freedom and desire to take strangers, as it were, into their bosom, as was enough

to make us forget all that was dear to us in our own
countries. And continually we met with many things
right worthy of observation and relation; as, indeed, if
there be a mirror in the world worthy to hold men's
eyes, it is that country. One day there were two of
our company bidden to a feast of the family, as they
call it; a most natural, pious, and reverend custom it
is, showing that nation to be compounded of all good-
ness. This is the manner of it: it is granted to any
man that shall live to see thirty persons descended of
his body alive together, and all above three years old,
to make this feast, which is done at the cost of the
State. The father of the family, whom they call the
Tirsan, two days before the feast, taketh to him three of
such friends as he liketh to choose, and is assisted also
by the governor of the city or place where the feast is
celebrated; and all the persons of the family of both
sexes are summoned to attend him. These two days
the Tirsan sitteth in consultation concerning the good
estate of the family. There, if there be any discord or
suits between any of the family, they are compounded
and appeased. There, if any of the family be distressed
or decayed, order is taken for their relief and compe-
tent means to live. There, if any be subject to vice, or
take ill courses, they are reproved and censured. So,
likewise, direction is given touching marriages, and
the courses of life which any of them should take, with
divers other the like orders and advices. The governor
assisteth to the end to put in execution by his public
authority the decrees and orders of the Tirsan if they

should be disobeyed, though that seldom needeth, such reverence and obedience they give to the order of nature. The Tirsan doth also then ever choose one man from amongst his sons to live in house with him, who is called ever after the Son of the Vine—the reason will hereafter appear. On the feast-day the father, or Tirsan, cometh forth after divine service into a large room, where the feast is celebrated, which room hath a half-pace at the upper end. Against the wall, in the middle of the half-pace, is a chair placed for him, with a table and carpet before it. Over the chair is a state, made round or oval, and it is of ivy—an ivy somewhat whiter than ours, like the leaf of a silver asp,* but more shining, for it is green all winter. And the state is curiously wrought with silver and silk of divers colours, broiding or binding in the ivy, and is ever of the work of some of the daughters of the family, and veiled over at the top with a fine net of silk and silver; but the substance of it is true ivy, whereof, after it is taken down, the friends of the family are desirous to have some leaf or sprig to keep. The Tirsan cometh forth with all his generation or lineage, the males before him and the females following him; and if there be a mother from whose body the whole lineage is descended, there is a traverse† placed in a loft above, on the right hand of

---

* *Asp*, aspen. First English, "æsp." *Aspen* is its adjective.

† *Traverse*, barrier or movable screen, sometimes formed only by a curtain.

the chair, with a privy door, and a carved window of glass leaded with gold and blue, where she sitteth, but is not seen. When the Tirsan is come forth he sitteth down in the chair, and all the lineage place themselves against the wall, both at his back and upon the return of the half-pace,* in order of their years, without difference of sex, and stand upon their feet. When he is set, the room being always full of company, but well kept and without disorder, after some pause there cometh in from the lower end of the room a taratan (which is as much as a herald), and on either side of him two young lads, whereof one carrieth a scroll of their shining yellow parchment, and the other a cluster of grapes of gold, with a long foot, or stalk. The herald and children are clothed with mantles of sea-water green satin, but the herald's mantle is streamed with gold, and hath a train. Then the herald, with three curtseys, or rather inclinations, cometh up as far as the half-pace, and there first taketh into his hand the scroll. This scroll is the king's charter, containing gift of revenue, and many privileges, exemptions, and points of honour granted to the father of the family; and it is ever styled and directed: "To such an one, our Well-beloved Friend and Creditor," which is a title

* *The return of the half-pace.* *Return* is here used in the architectural sense of the continuation of a moulding, projection, &c., in a contrary direction; a part that falls away from the front of a straight work; as here the *half-pace* (the raised floor or scaffold), projects from the straight line of the wall.

proper only to this case. For they say, the king is debtor to no man but for propagation of his subjects. The seal set to the king's charter is the king's image embossed, or moulded, in gold; and though such charters be expedited of course, and as of right, yet they are varied by discretion, according to the number and dignity of the family. This charter the herald readeth aloud, and while it is read the father, or Tirsan, standeth up, supported by two of his sons, such as he chooseth. Then the herald mounteth the half-pace, and delivereth the charter into his hand, and with that there is an acclamation by all that are present in their language, which is thus much, "Happy are the people of Bensalem." Then the herald taketh into his hand from the other child the cluster of grapes, which is of gold, both the stalk and the grapes. But the grapes are daintily enamelled; and if the males of the family be the greater number, the grapes are enamelled purple, with a little sun set on the top; if the females, then they are enamelled into a greenish-yellow, with a crescent on the top. The grapes are in number as many as there are descendants of the family. This golden cluster the herald delivereth also to the Tirsan, who presently delivereth it over to that son that he had formerly chosen to be in house with him, who beareth it before his father as an ensign of honour when he goeth in public ever after, and is thereupon called the Son of the Vine.

After this ceremony ended, the father, or Tirsan, re-tireth, and after some time cometh forth again to dinner, where he sitteth alone under the state as before, and none of his descendants sit with him of what degree or dignity soever, except he hap to be of Salomon's House. He is served only by his own children, such as are male, who perform unto him all service of the table upon the knee; and the women only stand about him, leaning against the wall. The room below the half-pace hath tables on the sides for the guests that are bidden, who are served with great and comely order. And towards the end of dinner (which, in the greatest feast with them, lasteth never above an hour and a half) there is a hymn sung, varied according to the invention of him that composeth it (for they have excellent poesy), but the subject of it is always the praises of Adam, and Noah, and Abraham, whereof the former two peopled the world, and the last was the Father of the Faithful: concluding ever with a thanksgiving for the Nativity of our Saviour, in whose birth the births of all are only blessed. Dinner being done, the Tirsan retireth again, and having withdrawn himself alone into a place, where he maketh some private prayers, he cometh forth the third time to give the blessing, with all his descendants, who stand about him as at the first. Then he calleth them forth by one and by one, by name, as he pleaseth, though seldom the order of age be inverted. The person that is called (the table being before removed) kneeleth down before the chair, and the father layeth his hand upon his head, or her head, and giveth the blessing in these words: "Son of Bensalem [or daughter of Bensalem], thy father saith it : the man by whom thou hast breath and life speaketh the word ; the blessing of the Everlasting Father, the Prince of Peace, and the Holy Dove be upon thee, and make the days of thy pilgrimage good and many." This he saith to every one of them ; and that done, if there be any of his sons of eminent merit and virtue (so they be not above two), he calleth for them again, and saith, laying his arm over their shoulders, they standing, " Sons, it is well ye are born ; give God the praise, and persevere to the end."   And withal delivereth to either of them a jewel, made in the figure of an ear of wheat, which they ever after wear in the front of their turban, or hat.   This done, they fall to music and dances, and other recreations after their manner for the rest of the day.   This is the full order of that feast.

By that time six or seven days were spent, I was fallen into straight acquaintance with a merchant of that city, whose name was Joabin. He was a Jew, and circumcised, for they have some few stirps* of Jews yet remaining among them, whom they leave to their own religion : which they may the better do because they are of a far different disposition from the Jews in other parts : for whereas they hate the name of Christ, and have a secret inbred rancour against the people amongst whom they live, these, contrariwise, give unto our Saviour many high attributes, and love the nation of Bensalem extremely. Surely this man of whom I

* *Stirps*. See Note, p. 153.

speak would ever acknowledge that Christ was born of
a virgin, and that He was more than a man; and he
would tell how God made Him ruler of the seraphims
which guard His throne; and they call him also the
Milken Way, and the Elijah of the Messiah, and many
other high names, which, though they be inferior to
His Divine Majesty, yet they are far from the language of other Jews. And for the country of Bensalem this man would make no end of commending it,
being desirous by tradition among the Jews there to
have it believed that the people thereof were of the
generations of Abraham by another son, whom they
called Nachoran; and that Moses by a secret cabala
ordained the laws of Bensalem which they now use;
and that when the Messiah should come, and sit in His
throne at Jerusalem, the king of Bensalem should sit
at his feet, whereas other kings should keep a great
distance. But yet, setting aside these Jewish dreams,
the man was a wise man, and learned, and of great
policy, and excellently seen in * the laws and customs
of that nation. Amongst other discourses one day, I
told him I was much affected with the relation I had
from some of the company of their custom in holding
the Feast of the Family, for that, methought I had
never heard of a solemnity wherein Nature did so much
preside. And I desired to know of him what laws
and customs they had concerning marriage, and

---

* *Seen in*, skilled in. Imitation of the Latin use of " spec-
tatus ; " a common phrase in Old English.

whether they kept marriage well, and whether they were tied to one wife; for that where population is so much affected, and such as with them it seemed to be, there is commonly permission of plurality of wives. To this he said, "You have reason to commend that excellent institution of the Feast of the Family, and, indeed, we have experience that those families that are partakers of the blessing of that feast do flourish and prosper ever after in an extraordinary manner. But hear me now, and I will tell you what I know. You shall understand that there is not under the heavens so chaste a nation as this of Bensalem, nor so free from all pollution or foulness. It is the virgin of the world. I remember I have read in one of your European books of a holy hermit amongst you that desired to see the spirit of fornication, and there appeared to him a little, foul, ugly Ethiop; but if he had desired to see the spirit of chastity of Bensalem, it would have appeared to him in the likeness of a fair, beautiful cherubim; for there is nothing amongst mortal men more fair and admirable than the chaste minds of this people. Know, therefore, that with them there are no stews, no dissolute houses, no courtesans, nor anything of that kind. Nay, they wonder, with detestation, at you in Europe which permit such things. They say ye have put marriage out of office, for marriage is ordained a remedy for unlawful concupiscence; and natural concupiscence seemeth as a spur to marriage; but when men have at hand a remedy more agreeable to their corrupt will, marriage

is almost expulsed. And, therefore, there are with you
seen infinite men that marry not, but choose rather a
libertine and impure single life than to be yoked in
marriage; and many that do marry, marry late, when
the prime and strength of their years are past. And
when they do marry, what is the marriage to them but
a very bargain, wherein is sought alliance, or portion,
or reputation, with some desire (almost indifferent) of
issue, and not the faithful nuptial union of man and
wife that was first instituted. Neither is it possible
that those that have cast away so basely so much of
their strength should greatly esteem children (being of
the same matter) as chaste men do. So likewise, during marriage, is the case much amended, as it ought to
be if those things were tolerated only for necessity?
No, but they remain still as a very affront to marriage.
The haunting of those dissolute places, or resort to
courtesans, are no more punished in married men than
in bachelors, and the depraved custom of change, and
the delight in meretricious embracements (where sin is
turned into art), maketh marriage a dull thing, and a
kind of imposition, or tax. They hear you defend
these things as done to avoid greater evils; but they
say this is a preposterous wisdom, and they call it
Lot's offer, who, to save his guests, offered his
daughters. Nay, they say further that there is little
gained in this, for that the same vices and appetites do
still remain and abound: unlawful lust being like a
furnace, that if you stop the flames altogether, it will
quench; but if you give it any vent, it will rage. As

for masculine love, they have no touch of it: and yet there are not so faithful and inviolate friendships in the world again as are there; and to speak generally, as I said before, I have not read of any such chastity in any people as theirs. And their usual saying is, ' That whosover is unchaste cannot reverence himself.' And they say, ' That the reverence of a man's self is, next religion, the chiefest bridle of all vices.' " And when he had said this, the good Jew paused a little; whereupon I, far more willing to hear him speak on than to speak myself, yet thinking it decent that upon his pause of speech I should not be altogether silent, said only this, " That I would say to him as the widow of Sarepta said to Elias: that he was come to bring to memory our sins, and that I confess the righteousness of Bensalem was greater than the righteousness of Europe." At which speech he bowed his head, and went on in this manner: " They have also many wise and excellent laws touching marriage; they allow no polygamy; they have ordained that none do intermarry or contract until a month be past from their first interview. Marriage without consent of parents they do not make void; but they mulct in the inheritors, for the children of such marriages are not admitted to inherit above a third part of their parents' inheritance."

And as we were thus in conference there came one that seemed to be a messenger, in a rich huke,* that

* *Huke,* cloak. Old French "huque." Probably named from the piece of cotton cloth worn by the Arabs over the

spake with the Jew, whereupon he turned to me, and said : "You will pardon me, for I am commanded away in haste." The next morning he came to me again, joyful as it seemed, and said : "There is word come to the governor of the city that one of the fathers of Salomon's House will be here this day seven-night. We have seen none of them these dozen years; his coming is in state; but the cause of his coming is secret. I will provide you and your fellows of a good standing to see his entry." I thanked him, and told him I was most glad of the news. The day being come, he made his entry. He was a man of middle stature and age, comely of person, and had an aspect as if he pitied men. He was clothed in a robe of fine black cloth, with wide sleeves and a cape; his under-garment was of excellent white linen, down to the foot, girt with a girdle of the same, and a sindon,* or tippet, of the same about his neck. He had gloves that were curious and set with stone; and shoes of peach-coloured velvet; his neck was bare to the shoulders; his hat was like a helmet, or Spanish montera; † and his locks curled below it decently (they were of colour brown); his beard was cut round, and of the same colour with his hair, but somewhat lighter. He was carried in a rich chariot without wheels,

tunic, *haik*, from Ar. "haka," to weave. The word occurs in Old English as *haik*, *hyke*, and *huke*.

 * *Sindon.* See Note, page 149.

 † *Montera*, a hunting-cap, from "montero," a huntsman, so called because his game is on the mountain, "monte."

litterwise, with two horses at either end, richly trapped in blue velvet embroidered, and two footmen on each side in the like attire. The chariot was all of cedar, gilt, and adorned with crystal, save that the fore-end had panels of sapphires set in borders of gold, and the hinder end the like of emeralds of the Peru colour; there was also a sun of gold, radiant upon the top, in the midst, and on the top before, a small cherub of gold with wings displayed. The chariot was covered with cloth of gold tissued upon blue. He had before him fifty attendants, young men all, in white satin loose coats to the mid leg, and stockings of white silk, and shoes of blue velvet, and hats of blue velvet, with fine plumes of divers colours set round like hat-bands. Next before the chariot went two men, bare-headed, in linen garments down to the foot, girt, and shoes of blue velvet, who carried the one a crosier, the other a pastoral staff, like a sheep-hook, neither of them of metal, but the crosier of balm-wood, the pastoral staff of cedar. Horsemen he had none, neither before nor behind his chariot, as it seemeth, to avoid all tumult and trouble. Behind his chariot went all the officers and principals of the companies of the city. He sat alone upon cushions of a kind of excellent plush, blue; and under his foot curious carpets of silk of divers colours, like the Persian, but far finer. He held up his bare hand, as he went, as blessing the people, but in silence. The street was wonderfully well kept, so that there was never any army had their men stand in better battle array than the people stood. The windows likewise were not crowded, but every one stood in them as if they had been placed. When the show was passed the Jew said to me, " I shall not be able to attend you as I would, in regard of some charge the city hath laid upon me for the entertaining of this great person." Three days after, the Jew came to me again, and said, " Ye are happy men, for the father of Salomon's House taketh knowledge of your being here, and commanded me to tell you that he will admit all your company to his presence, and have private conference with one of you that ye shall choose, and for this hath appointed the next day after to-morrow; and because he meaneth to give you his blessing he hath appointed it in the forenoon." We came at our day and hour, and I was chosen by my fellows for the private access. We found him in a fair chamber, richly hanged, and carpeted under foot, without any degrees to the state;* he was sat upon a low throne richly adorned, and a rich cloth of state over his head of blue satin embroidered. He was alone, save that he had two pages of honour on each hand, one finely attired in white; his under garments were the like that we saw him wear in the chariot, but instead of his gown he had on him a mantle with a cape, of the same fine black, fastened about him. When we came in, as we were taught, we bowed low at our first entrance; and when we were come near his chair he stood up, holding forth his hand ungloved, and in posture of blessing, and we,

---

* *Degrees to the state,* steps up to the canopied seat.

every one of us, stooped down and kissed the hem of his tippet; that done, the rest departed, and I remained. Then he warned the pages forth of the room, and caused me to sit down beside him, and spake to me thus in the Spanish tongue :—

"God bless thee, my son! I will give thee the greatest jewel I have, for I will impart unto thee, for the love of God and men, a relation of the true state of Salomon's House. Son, to make you know the true state of Salomon's House, I will keep this order: first, I will set forth unto you the end of our foundation. Secondly, the preparations and instruments we have for our works. Thirdly, the several employments and functions whereto our fellows are assigned. And, fourthly, the ordinances and rites which we observe.

"The end of our foundation is the knowledge of causes, and secret motions of things; and the enlarging of the bounds of human empire, to the effecting of all things possible.*

"The preparations and instruments are these: we have large and deep caves of several depths; the deepest are sunk six hundred fathoms, and some of them are dug and made under great hills and mountains, so that if you reckon together the depth of the hill and the depth of the cave, they are (some of them) above three miles deep. For we find that the depth of a hill and the depth of a cave from the flat is the same

---

* *The end of our foundation* was the avowed aim of the whole system of Bacon's philosophy.

thing; both remote alike from the sun and heaven's beams, and from the open air. Those caves we call the lower region, and we use them for all coagulations, indurations, refrigerations, and conservations of bodies. We use them likewise for the imitation of natural mines, and the producing also of new artificial metals by compositions and materials which we use, and lay there for many years. We use them also sometimes (which may seem strange) for curing of some diseases, and for prolongation of life, in some hermits that choose to live there, well accommodated of all things necessary, and indeed live very long; by whom also we learn many things.

"We have burials in several earths, where we put divers cements, as the Chinese do their porcelain, but we have them in greater variety, and some of them more fine. We have also great variety of composts and soils for the making of the earth fruitful.

"We have high towers, the highest about half a mile in height, and some of them likewise set upon high mountains, so that the vantage of the hill with the tower is, in the highest of them, three miles at least. And these places we call the upper region; accounting the air between the high places and the low as a middle region. We use these towers, according to their several heights and situations, for insolation,* refrigeration, conservation, and for the view of divers meteors, as winds, rain, snow, hail, and some of the

---

* *Insolation*, exposing to the rays of the sun.

fiery meteors also. And upon them, in some places, are dwellings of hermits, whom we visit sometimes, and instruct what to observe.

"We have great lakes, both salt and fresh, whereof we have use for the fish and fowl. We use them also for burials of some natural bodies; for we find a difference in things buried in earth or in air below the earth, and things buried in water. We have also pools, of which some do strain fresh water out of salt, and others by art do turn fresh water into salt. We have also some rocks in the midst of the sea, and some bays upon the shore, for some works wherein are required the air and vapour of the sea. We have likewise violent streams and cataracts, which serve us for many motions, and likewise engines for multiplying and enforcing of winds, to set also on going diverse motions.

"We have also a number of artificial wells and fountains, made in imitation of the natural sources and baths, as tincted upon vitriol, sulphur, steel, brass, lead, nitre, and other minerals. And again, we have little wells for infusions of many things, where the waters take the virtue quicker and better than in vessels or basins. And amongst them we have a water which we call water of Paradise, being, by that we do to it, made very sovereign for health and prolongation of life.

"We have also great and spacious houses where we imitate and demonstrate meteors, as snow, hail, rain, some artificial rains of bodies and not of water, thunders, lightnings; also generations of bodies in air, as frogs, flies, and divers others.

"We have also certain chambers, which we call chambers of health, where we qualify the air as we think good and proper, for the cure of divers diseases and preservation of health.

"We have also fair and large baths of several mixtures, for the cure of diseases and the restoring of man's body from arefaction; * and others for the confirming of it in strength of sinews, vital parts, and the very juice and substance of the body.

"We have also large and various orchards and gardens, wherein we do not so much respect beauty as variety of ground and soil proper for divers trees and herbs, and some very spacious, where trees and berries are set, whereof we make divers kinds of drinks, besides the vineyards. In these we practise likewise all conclusions † of grafting and inoculating, as well of wild trees as fruit trees, which produceth many effects. And we make (by art) in the same orchards and gardens, trees and flowers to come earlier or later than their seasons, and to come up and bear more speedily than by their natural course they do. We make them also, by art, greater much than their nature, and their fruit greater and sweeter, and of differing taste,

---

* *Arefaction*, being made dry; from Latin "arere," to be dry, and "facere," to make.

† *Practise conclusions*, equivalent to "try conclusions," make the experiment from which conclusions may be drawn.

smell, colour, and figure from their nature. And many of them we so order as they become of medicinal use.

" We have also means to make divers plants rise by mixtures of earth without seeds, and likewise to make divers new plants, differing from the vulgar; and to make one tree or plant turn into another.

" We have also parks and enclosures of all sorts of beasts and birds, which we use not only for view or rareness, but likewise for dissections and trials, that thereby we may take light what may be wrought upon the body of man. Wherein we find many strange effects, as continuing life in them, though divers parts, which you account vital, be perished and taken forth; resuscitating of some that seem dead in appearance, and the like. We try, also, all poisons, and other medicines upon them, as well of chirurgery as physic. By art, likewise, we make them greater or taller than their kind is, and, contrariwise, dwarf them, and stay their growth; we make them more fruitful and bearing than their kind is, and, contrariwise, barren and not generative; also we make them differ in colour, shape, activity—many ways. We find means to make commixtures of divers kinds, which have produced many new kinds, and them not barren, as the general opinion is. We make a number of kinds of serpents, worms, flies, fishes, of putrefaction, whereof some are advanced (in effect) to be perfect creatures, like beasts or birds, and have sexes, and do propagate. Neither do we this by chance, but we know beforehand, of what matter and commixture, what kind of those creatures will arise.

"We have also particular pools, where we make trials upon fishes, as we have said before of beasts and birds.

"We have also places for breed and generation of those kinds of worms and flies which are of special use, such as are with you your silkworms and bees.

"I will not hold you long with recounting of our brewhouses, bakehouses, and kitchens, where are made divers drinks, breads, and meats, rare, and of special effects. Wines we have of grapes, and drinks of other juice of fruits, of grains, and of roots; and of mixtures with honey, sugar, manna, and fruits dried and decocted. Also of the tears and woundings of trees, and of the pulp of canes. And these drinks are of several ages, some to the age or last of forty years. We have drinks also brewed with several herbs, and roots, and spices; yea, with several fleshes and white meats, whereof some of the drinks are such as they are in effect meat and drink both, so that divers, especially in age, do desire to live with them, with little or no meat or bread. And, above all, we strive to have drinks of extreme thin parts, to insinuate into the body, and yet without all biting, sharpness, or fretting; insomuch as some of them, put upon the back of your hand, will, with a little stay, pass through to the palm, and yet taste mild to the mouth. We have also waters which we ripen in that fashion, as they become nourishing, so that they are indeed excellent drink, and many will use no other.   Breads we have of several grains, roots, and kernels: yea, and some of flesh and fish, dried, with divers kinds of leavenings and seasonings, so that some do extremely move appetites.   Some do nourish so as divers do live on them without any other meat, who live very long.   So for meats, we have some of them so beaten and made tender, and mortified, yet without all corrupting, as a weak heat of the stomach will turn them into good chylus, as well as a strong heat would meat otherwise prepared.   We have some meats also, and breads, and drinks, which, taken by men, enable them to fast long after; and some other, that used make the very flesh of men's bodies sensibly more hard and tough, and their strength far greater than otherwise it would be.

"We have dispensatories, or shops of medicines, wherein you may easily think, if we have such variety of plants and living creatures more than you have in Europe—for we know what you have—the simples, drugs, and ingredients of medicines must likewise be in so much the greater variety.   We have them, likewise, of divers ages and long fermentations; and for their preparations we have not only all manner of exquisite distillations and separations, and especially by gentle heats, and percolations through divers strainers, yea, and substances; but also exact forms of composition, whereby they incorporate almost as they were natural simples.

"We have also divers mechanical arts which you have not, and stuffs made by them, as papers, linen, silks, tissues, dainty works of feathers of wonderful lustre, excellent dyes, and many others; and shops, likewise, as well for such as are not brought into vulgar use amongst us, as for those that are; for you must know that of the things before recited, many of them are grown into use throughout the kingdom; but yet if they did flow from our invention, we have of them also for patterns and principals.

"We have also furnaces of great diversities, and that keep great diversity of heats, fierce and quick, strong and constant, soft and mild, blown, quiet, dry, moist, and the like; but above all we have heats in imitation of the sun's and heavenly bodies' heats, that pass divers inequalities, and, as it were, orbs, progresses, and returns, whereby we produce admirable effects. Besides, we have heats of dungs, and of bellies and maws of living creatures, and of their bloods and bodies; and of hays and herbs laid up moist, of lime unquenched, and such like. Instruments, also, which generate heat only by motion. And further, places for strong insolations; and again, places under the earth, which, by nature of art, yield heat. These divers heats we use as the nature of the operation which we intend requireth.

"We have, also, perspective houses, where we make demonstrations of all lights and radiations, and of all colours; and out of things uncoloured and transparent we can represent unto you all several colours, not in rainbows—as it is in gems and prisms—but of themselves single. We represent, also, all multiplications of light, which we carry to great distance, and make so sharp as to discern small points and lines. Also all colourations of light; all delusions and deceits of the sight, in figures, magnitudes, motions, colours; all demonstrations of shadows. We find, also, divers means yet unknown to you of producing of light originally from divers bodies. We procure means of seeing objects afar off, as in the heaven, and remote places; and represent things near as afar off, and things afar off as near, making feigned distances. We have also helps for the sight, far above spectacles and glasses in use; we have also glasses and means to see small and minute bodies perfectly and distinctly, as the shapes and colours of small flies and worms, grains and flaws in gems, which cannot otherwise be seen; observations in urine and blood not otherwise to be seen. We make artificial rainbows, halos, and circles about light; we represent also all manner of reflections, refractions, and multiplications of visual beams of objects.

"We have also precious stones of all kinds, many of them of great beauty, and to you unknown; crystals likewise, and glasses of divers kinds. And amongst them some of metals vitrificated, and other materials, besides those of which you make glass. Also a number of fossils and imperfect minerals, which you have not. Likewise loadstones of prodigious virtue, and other rare stones, both natural and artificial.

"We have also sound-houses, where we practise and demonstrate all sounds, and their generation. We have harmonies which you have not, of quarter-sounds and lesser slides of sounds. Divers instruments of music, likewise to you unknown, some sweeter than any you have, together with bells and rings that are dainty and sweet. We represent small sounds as great and deep, likewise great sounds extenuate and sharp; we make divers tremblings and warblings of sounds which in their original are entire. We represent and imitate all articulate sounds and letters, and the voices and notes of beasts and birds. We have certain helps, which, set to the ear, do further the hearing greatly. We have also divers strange and artificial echoes, reflecting the voice many times, and, as it were, tossing it; and some that give back the voice louder than it came, some shriller, and some deeper. Yea, some rendering the voice, differing in the letters or articulate sound from that they receive. We have also means to convey sounds in trunks and pipes, in strange lines and distances.

"We have also perfume-houses, wherewith we join also practices of taste. We multiply smells, which may seem strange. We imitate smells, making all smells to breathe out of other mixtures than those that give them. We make divers imitations of taste likewise, so that they will deceive any man's taste. And in this house we contain also a confiture house, where we make all sweetmeats, dry and moist; and divers pleasant wines, milks, broths, and salads, far in greater variety than you have.

"We have also engine-houses, where are prepared

engines and instruments for all sorts of motions : there
we imitate and practise to make swifter motions than
any you have, either out of your muskets or any engine
that you have; and to make them and multiply them
more easily, and with small force, by wheels and other
means; and to make them stronger and more violent
than yours are, exceeding your greatest cannons and
basilisks. We represent, also, ordnance and instruments of war, and engines of all kinds; and likewise
new mixtures and compositions of gunpowder, wildfires
burning in water, and unquenchable; also fireworks of
all variety, both for pleasure and use.   We imitate, also,
flights of birds; we have some degrees of flying in the
air; we have ships and boats for going under water and
brooking of seas; also swimming-girdles and supporters. We have divers curious clocks, and other like
motions of return, and some perpetual motions. We
imitate also motions of living creatures, by images of
men, beasts, birds, fishes, and serpents. We have also a
great number of other various motions, strange for
equality, fineness, and subtlety.

"We have also a mathematical house, where are
represented all instruments, as well of geometry as
astronomy, exquisitely made.

"We have also houses of deceits of the senses, where
we represent all manner of feats of juggling, false
apparitions, impostures, and illusions, and their fallacies.
And surely you will easily believe that we that have so
many things truly natural which induce admiration,
could, in a world of particulars, deceive the senses, if

we would disguise those things, and labour to make them seem more miraculous. But we do hate all impostures and lies; insomuch as we have severely forbidden it to all our fellows, under pain of ignominy and fines, that they do not show any natural work or thing adorned or swelling, but only pure as it is, and without all affectation of strangeness.

"These are, my son, the riches of Salomon's House.

"For the several employments and offices of our fellows: We have twelve that sail into foreign countries under the names of other nations (for our own we conceal), who bring us the books, and abstracts, and patterns of experiments of all other parts. These we call Merchants of Light.

"We have three that collect the experiments which are in all books. These we call Depredators.

"We have three that collect the experiments of all mechanical arts, and also of liberal sciences, and also of practices which are not brought into arts. These we call Mystery men.

"We have three that try new experiments such as themselves think good. These we call Pioneers or Miners.

"We have three that draw the experiments of the former four into titles and tables, to give the better light for the drawing of observations and axioms out of them. These we call Compilers.

"We have three that bend themselves, looking into the experiments of their fellows, and casting about how to draw out of them things of use and practice for man's life and knowledge, as well for works as for plain demonstration of causes, means of natural divinations, and the easy and clear discovery of the virtues and parts of bodies. These we call Dowry-men, or Benefactors.

"Then after divers meetings and consults of our whole number, to consider of the former labours and collections, we have three that take care out of them to direct new experiments of a higher light, more penetrating into nature than the former. These we call Lamps.

"We have three others that do execute the experiments so directed, and report them. These we call Inoculators.

"Lastly, we have three that raise the former discoveries, by experiments, into greater observations, axioms, and aphorisms. These we call Interpreters of Nature.

"We have also, as you must think, novices and apprentices, that the succession of the former employed men do not fail, besides a great number of servants and attendants—men and women. And this we do also: we have consultations which of the inventions and experiences which we have discovered shall be published, and which not; and take all an oath of secrecy for concealing of those which we think fit to keep secret, though some of those we do reveal sometimes to the State, and some not.

"For our ordinances and rites, we have two very long

and fair galleries : in one of these we place patterns and samples of all manner of the more rare and excellent inventions; in the other we place the statues of the principal inventors. There we have the statue of your Columbus, that discovered the West Indies; also the inventor of ships ; your Monk, that was the inventor of ordnance and of gunpowder; the inventor of music; the inventor of letters; the inventor of printing; the inventor of observations of astronomy; the inventor of works in metal; the inventor of glass; the inventor of silk of the worm; the inventor of wine; the inventor of corn and bread; the inventor of sugars; and all these by more certain tradition than you have. Then have we divers inventors of our own of excellent works, which, since you have not seen, it were too long to make descriptions of them; and besides, in the right understanding of those descriptions, you might easily err; for upon every invention of value we erect a statue to the inventor, and give him a liberal and honourable reward. These statues are, some of brass, some of marble and touchstone,* some of cedar and other special woods, gilt and adorned, some of iron, some of silver, and some of gold.

"We have certain hymns and services, which we say daily, of laud and thanks to God for His marvellous works, and forms of prayers imploring His aid and

*Touchstone, Lydian stone, or basanite, is silicious schist, almost as compact as flint, called touchstone because it was used to indicate the purity of gold by the streak left where the gold had been drawn across it.

blessing for the illumination of our labours, and the turning of them into good and holy uses.

"Lastly, we have circuits, or visits, of divers principal cities of the kingdom, where, as it cometh to pass, we do publish such new profitable inventions as we think good. And we do also declare natural divinations of diseases, plagues, swarms of hurtful creatures, scarcity, tempests, earthquakes, great inundations, comets, temperature of the year, and divers other things; and we give counsel thereupon what the people shall do for the prevention and remedy of them."

And when he had said this, he stood up. And I, as I had been taught, kneeled down, and he laid his right hand upon my head, and said:—"God bless thee, my son; and God bless this relation which I have made. I give thee leave to publish it, for the good of other nations; for we here are in God's bosom, a land unknown." And so he left me, having assigned a value of about two thousand ducats for a bounty to me and my fellows. For they give great largesses when they come, upon all occasions.

The rest was not perfected.

Printed by Cassell & Company, Limited, La Belle Sauvage, London, E.C.

www.ingramcontent.com/pod-product-compliance
Lightning Source LLC
Chambersburg PA
CBHW080331270326
41927CB00014B/3169